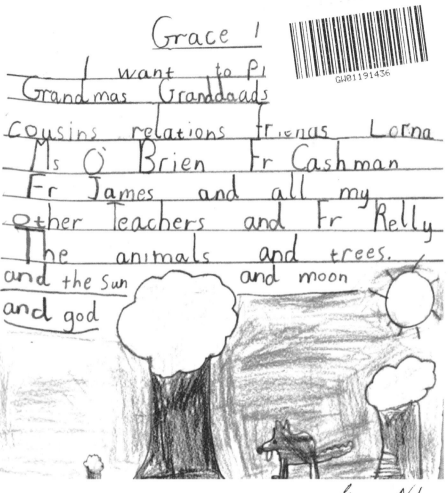

Grace 1

I want to pi
Grandmas Granddaads
cousins relations friends Lorna
Ms O Brien Fr Cashman
Fr James and all my
other Teachers and Fr Relly
The animals and trees.
and the sun and moon
and god

Grace Nolan
AGED 8

Dear Grace

by
Children of Ireland

2003

Published by the Grace Nolan Foundation Ltd.
Limited by Guarantee.

Acknowledgements

I wrote in last year's first collection of "Dear Grace " letters that it was impossible to list the sheer volume of friends, professionals, medical staff and perfect strangers that have come into our lives since the passing of Grace, our darling daughter. It is a great comfort to our family that our efforts to ensure Grace did not die in vain are recognised, understood, and in some cases the motivating factor in bringing willing volunteers to our cause and it's ideals.

To my amazing wife June and our wonderful children, thank you for affording me the time and freedom to remember Grace in this way, and for all your help and support through difficult times.My love to you always.

To my dear friend Brendan O'Carroll, who again this year as for the last four years has given his support & time unconditionally, and for the simple and sole reward of furthering the Foundation along the road of it's ideals. Brendan, there are no words I can write that can truly describe my gratitude to one of God's great human creations, save to say that you have inspired me and I love you.

To run the "Dear Grace" letter competition and compile the "Dear Grace 2003" book a lot of help was required and I am very grateful to Harry and Pauline Delaney who organised and co-ordinated the competition, prepared and sent out the entry forms, liaised with all the teachers and schools, and worked long hours with the selection committee to read all the thousands of letters. Thank you so much.

For his patience in editing and proofing and for helping me compile this year's book, (and for correcting my spellings) I thank my dear friend Mick Mulcahy. Thank you to Clyde Carroll and Karl Rogers for helping co-ordinate with our promotion team and John Fagan of Future Print our printers in Dublin.

To Stuart Campbell at Graphic Design, Cork, for his co-operation and patience in helping me complete this years book, to Collette Nolan, Billy Foley, Andrew Boyle, Mick O'Shea and Irene Murphy for their wonderful illustrations to the children's stories, and their encouragement to get Grace's own siblings, Aimee, Ryan, Dean & Eva to draw for the book, I send my heartfelt gratitude.

To each and every Irish child who put pen to paper to write to their Heavenly pen friend, Grace, and to each and every teacher and parent who encouraged our scribes,
I thank you most sincerely.

Our new website **www.gracenolan.com** is now up and running, and I thank my colleague Ray Crowley for his efforts in this regard. You can e-mail us at **info@gracenolan.com**

Thank you to **Datacom Eireann Teoranta** of Clonakilty & Portlaoise who were delighted to sponsor 21 **iQon Computers** which were supplied to the winning schools, and to the manufacturers, iQon Technologies [the No 1 indigenous PC manufacturer in Ireland]. Check out **www.iqon-computers.com**
To Musgraves and Coca Cola who so kindly assisted in the remainder of the prizes the children enjoyed your generosity and you have our thanks.

To my long time friends Robin Noonan of BN Insurances, Cork, and Tom and Barbara Coakley, your generosity to The Grace Nolan Foundation often goes unpublicised but is deeply appreciated.
To Keith Duffy, I am so happy to have you as a friend and now welcome you as a patron to the Foundation I look forward to working with you in 2004.

For applying their nimble fingers in getting the winning stories typeset, I thank Dara O'Mahony and Niambh McGarry of Active HealthCare and QEF Global respectively.

I thank you all,
Mike Nolan

Typeset by Graphic Design, Cork
Cover photograph by Healy Rimmington, Cork
Cover and Contents Printed and Bound in Ireland by Future Print, Baldoyle, Dublin

Edited by Mike Nolan.

To Grace ...

Introduction

Hi there and welcome to Dear Grace 2003 !

This is our second edition and if it should prove anything like our first we will be delighted. The short life and tragic passing of Grace Nolan has inspired children all over Ireland to put pen to paper yet again, and share with us their hilarious, shocking and very important view of the year just gone. They have allowed us into their lives and within these pages they share with us their deepest thoughts. It has been a pleasure and indeed a privilege to do this.

Let me congratulate the winners of this years Dear Grace Awards. I hope you enjoyed the awards ceremony in Dublin and I hope you are receiving the proper recognition and thanks from your school for winning them a fab computer. (No home work for at least two weeks?)

I would like to also say something to the many thousands of you whom were not selected for this years book. You are FANTASTIC. We have read EVERY story and letter that came to us. Believe me when I tell you that we could have published twenty books for we had so many wonderful letters to Grace. But alas, we must keep it to the ones that are here in the one book we have. Although you did not win this year, let me tell you what you have done. You have saved lives! You have made a huge contribution to the families and friend of sufferers of HHT. And you made me smile, thank you for that. You have also inspired all of us involved to keep this wonderful event going for as long as we can, and our lives are so much richer for getting your letters.

So, go on then, open the pages and enjoy history from the mouths of Irelands greatest asset, our children. We love you all.

Brendan O'Carroll

Dublin 2003

Foreword

Hello, and thank you so much to all the wonderful children for their letters to Dear Grace, and to all the teachers and parents who helped and encouraged them to write.

The children were asked to review 2003 through their eyes and minds, and what a beautiful snapshot in time they have produced, covering local and global events with passion, humour and clarity.

The Grace Nolan Foundation intends to publish a book by the children of Ireland in this format annually, and for as long as we can afford to do so.

The book's primary purpose is to raise money to combat HHT globally, and to fund the National HHT Centre in Cork. Its other purpose is to inspire children to write and participate in reviewing the year, recording history, and of course, having fun in doing so.

It will be interesting to see how the future books evolve as we record the decade, and when we look back, the children will have created a valuable and interesting review.

So, let me tell you what the Grace Nolan Foundation has achieved with your help in 2003.

It has indeed been a hectic year. It really began in December 2002, with the launch of the "Dear Grace Book 2002" on the Late Late Show. On the show, we signalled our intention to open the first National HHT Centre, to treat and screen HHT patients in Ireland. The good news is, that we opened the centre in April 2003 at the Mercy University Hospital in Cork, and Minister for Health & Children Micheal Martin TD, at the official opening ceremony, awarded the centre a €50,000 Capital Grant, and an annual allowance of €20,000 to defray running costs.

In 2003, The Grace Nolan Foundation also contributed almost €50,000 to the new centre toward the purchase of medical and office equipment, and to fund the appointment of a dedicated patient co-ordinator to enhance the service between the hospital and the patients.

As the only European board member of HHT Foundation International Inc., I attended the annual HHT World conference in the USA. News of the Irish HHT Centre's opening was well received, and it gave me great pleasure on behalf of the Grace Nolan Foundation, to present a cheque for $15,000 to further the global genetic research programme.

On 6th November, to thank the children who took part in the writing competition, we created the first annual "Dear Grace Awards", which took place at Dublin's Olympia Theatre. There, we met and rewarded the winners, whose literary efforts make up the book which is now in your hands. Those who won an award, brought their classmates and teachers, and over a thousand children filled the theatre ! Schools from all over Ireland attended, travelling from as far away as Cork, Kerry and Monaghan! What a great Day. They saw pop bands perform, met celebrity presenters, drank minerals and scoffed sweets and even had a video link from Dustin and the gang on the Den TV show ! Better than the Oscars or what ? I hope those who attended enjoyed themselves!

Foreword

A special thanks to Clyde Carroll for organising & co-ordinating the Dear Grace Awards. Clyde, you made my family and I very proud. To the presenters, my dear friends Brendan O'Carroll and Jennifer Gibney, thank you both for rehearsing tirelessly in the kitchen, and to all the hard working team at BOC Productions for their time, love and support. Thanks to the celebrities and friends and sponsors that contributed to the day and a final thanks to Denis Desmond, Caroline Downey and Brian Whitehead for their generosity and use of the Olympia Theatre. You really helped make it a day to remember for us all, especially the children.

Now children, don't forget to write and please spread the word, because we are going to do it all again next year. We thank you for buying this book. All proceeds from the sale of this book, will, I promise, be put to similar good use in 2004.

Because of the "Dear Grace" projects, including this book, over 100 HHT consultations have taken place and more than a dozen operations have been successfully undertaken which have ultimately saved lives, or at least dramatically improved them. Under the stewardship of Medical Director, Dr. Adrian Brady, and patient co-ordinator, Dr. Margaret Murphy, the National H.H.T. Centre is making great progress. Thanks in no small way to the efforts of the young aspiring writers and all who purchase this publication annually, the raised awareness of the condition have given many Irish people new and indeed, renewed hope.
We promise to maintain every effort to highlight and combat the HHT condition and salute your assistance.

MIKE NOLAN
Chairman
Grace Nolan Foundation Ltd

Should you wish to contact the Centre for medical purposes, please contact,
The National HHT Centre,
Mercy University Hospital,
Cork.
Tele; 021-2305040   e-mail info@hht.ie
Website www.hht.ie

Should you wish to contact the Grace Nolan Foundation ltd, please contact,
The Grace Nolan Foundation
Units 11A & B, City link Park, Forge Hill,
Cork.
Tele; 021-4322401   e-mail info@gracenolan.com
www.gracenolan.com
Charitable donations to The Grace Nolan Foundation, a non profit organisation, can be made payable to the Grace Nolan Foundation Ltd., and sent to the above address.
The Foundation's charity registration number is CHY 14869.

Dedication

To our darling little girl Grace, Brendan O'Carroll and the Children of Ireland, who continue to inspire, and bring out the very best in people . . .

When I hear Louis Armstrong sing "Wonderful World" I always imagine he sings "Wonderful Girl" especially for you, Grace . . .

I see trees of green, red roses too
I see them bloom for me and you
And I think to myself what a wonderful world.

I see skies of blue and clouds of white
The bright blessed day, the dark sacred night
And I think to myself what a wonderful world.

The colours of the rainbow so pretty in the sky
Are also on the faces of people going by
I see friends shaking hands saying how do you do
They're really saying I love you.

I hear babies crying, I watch them grow
They'll learn much more than I'll ever know
And I think to myself what a wonderful world
Yes, I think to myself what a wonderful world.

Love and best wishes

Michael, June and family.

Letters to Grace ...

Dear Grace:

My name is Emma Waldron. How are you doing up there in heaven? Is it nice up there? How is the weather? I suppose it is nice because you are above clouds and it can't rain. My job is to tell you what has been going on down here on earth since you left.

Well first of all I went into 6th class. My new teacher Mrs Bolger is really, really nice. My dad said if your teacher is nice it is easy to learn and I have learned loads since I've been in her class.
The program "Friends" is over, unfortunately and Britney Spears is no longer singing. Let me think… Oh yes! They have built a new school here in Tralee. It is called Mounthawk although a lot of people call it Mountjoy (in reference to the prison) because it is a secondary school. Ha! Ha! Oh! Before I continue I'll need to ask you a little favour, could you say hi to my Grand Dad? His name is Tony Waldron and my uncle whose name is Stephen O'Brien for me please.

There is a new thing now (well I am not so sure if it is new but this is the first time I've heard of it) called no car day. People are designing posters and making stories for it. I am designing a poster as well.

Have you met God yet? If so, what is he like? This is just my guess but I imagine him to be a big man with a long, white beard and a white flowing robe with a halo. Did you learn the meaning of life yet? I have so many questions but I will ask them later.

I guess you've already heard about the Twin Towers been blown up by Osama bin Laden, but did you know that President Bush has declared war and British soldiers have to fight as well? I'm really glad Ireland aren't involved because we are so small we would be squashed like teeny tiny bugs.

A new Harry Potter book came out called, "Order of the Phoenix". As far as I know it has sold millions of copies and has made millions of euros. Did you know that J.K. Rowling the author of Harry Potter books is so successful that she is richer than the Queen of England! She must be really, really rich.

The latest Coca-cola ad is a chiwawa song and every day coming home from school a group of kids are always singing it and I think my eardrums will burst from it.

2

In soccer news David Beckham, Victoria Beckham and their two sons have moved from England to Madrid because David Beckham is no longer playing for Manchester United. He is now playing for one of the world's best soccer teams Real Madrid (Madrid won't be long throwing them back HA! HA! Just kidding).

On a more serious note, two girls from England went missing and I don't think they were found… so now you know that not only funny, boring and weird things have happened but also some very sad things. But don't keep feeling depressed because good things have happened too. Like the three hundred and something episode of the Simpsons has come out. Bart meets his hero Tony Hawks.

In other news Justin Timberlake is a huge hit now and has had many, many songs this year such as "Rock your Body", "Senorita" and "Work it" (featuring Nelly). Oh yes and "Cry me a River" which was based on his and Britney's break up. Now I will ask you some questions.

The girl that somebody told you about last year (the one who killed herself because she was being bullied and thought that nobody loved her) have you met her? If you have could you tell her I said <u>Hi!</u> With a capital H. My next question, is Jesus really like what all the books describe him as or is he different? (that is if you have met him of course). I shall tell you about the soaps (and I don't mean the kind you wash your hands with he! He!).

In Eastenders Alfie and Kat finally start dating but of course they break up. Nana Moon is having problems and Alfie has to get the doctor. Lisa is back to get Louise and she is trying to kill Phil with the help of Denis (Sharon's brother). Phil is now married to Kate and at Christmas Jamie died.

In Coronation Street Peter got arrested for bigamy. Richard tried to kill Gail, Sarah, David and Bethany and he drives the car into the water, but don't worry because they get away, but Richard died.

I will tell you some jokes now!
"Knock, Knock"
"Who's there?"
"Boo"
"Boo who?"
"No need to cry it is only a joke!" (ha! Ha!)

Here's another one.
What did the hedgehog say when he put his jacket on inside out?..... OUCH!
(He! He!) I would tell you more jokes but I don't really know any.

Do you like books? I love reading books at the moment I am reading the fifth
Harry Potter book. I am only on page 106 and there are seven hundred and
sixty-six pages so I will be reading for a long time. I also like Darren Shan
books they are by J.K. Rowling as well.

Do you like porcelain dolls? I really really like them. I have six porcelain
dolls and one porcelain clown. Do you like teddies? I suppose you do. Nearly
everybody likes teddies, I've got a box full of them.

Do you think dolls are nice or do you hate them? I only like one doll it is a doll
that my Mom gave to me. It was my Mom's when she was about four and it is
older than you and me put together (it is pretty old, for a doll anyway). My
cousin hates dolls. She said she has grown out of them but she is only eight so I
don't see how.

Did you have any brothers or sisters? I have one sister called Lisa she is
thirteen she goes to secondary the one I told you about Mounthawk/Mountjoy.
She said it isn't bad but she would rather no school at all. I don't find school too
bad either because I have a nice teacher but I still would rather no school at all
as well. Is there a school up in heaven? If there is are the teachers nice, I guess
they are because it is heaven. I can't help wondering what it is like up in
heaven. I would love to meet God and spend the day in heaven. The only
problem is I would have to die first and I wasn't planning on doing that anytime
soon so I am stuck with dreaming and wondering for a while.

Do you miss your family? I bet you watch over them every day like their
guardian angel. I would miss my family if I were up in heaven. What is your
favourite program mine is the Simpsons and soaps and things like that.

I will be going to the cinema on Saturday to see "Underworld". It is a new
movie that is about a war between vampires and werewolves. I like movies
like that do you? I am sort of superstitious I believe in vampires. I wouldn't
want one to come into my house at night but I still believe in them. It is the
same with one of my best friends Jane Crean she believes in vampires and the
paranormal too.

4

Jane is ten. It was her birthday a couple of weeks ago. She had it in the cinema and then we went to Supermac's. In Supermac's we got balloons and we let them float up into the sky. They are probably with you up in heaven!

It is ten past eight now I have had my breakfast and I am ready for school but I don't have to go for a while so I decided to finish my letter to you. I am inside my sitting room now at the table writing and fiddling with my stamp and rubber. My sister got me them down town. The rubber is a burger with a rubber underneath and when you rub out the two eyes come popping out. The stamp is a fish with a stamp underneath and when you use the stamp the eyes pop out and it lights up. They are great fun to fiddle around with. Well I gotta go now Grace. I will see you someday but hopefully not someday too soon.

Bye Bye

Take Care

From your friend Emma Waldron,
Scoil Eoin, Balloonagh, Tralee,
Co. Kerry.

Dear Grace:

Hi, Stacey here. How are you? I'm fine. Isn't it a shame you dying and all. What age are you now? I'm going to be twelve in October. I can't wait, but I still don't know what to get and my mam keeps badgering me about it. I lost my phone while playing football. I got one off my aunt Catherine but it's a Motorola and not as good as my Nokia.

My aunt Bernadette got a new house a while ago. It's dreadful, first of all the back garden, it has millions of slugs and rubbish and the grass is way too long. Next are the bedrooms. They have a horrible cigarette smell, mouldy wallpaper. Cigarette burns on the carpet and beds and meldew on the windowsill. My other aunt Aisling bought a house in February and the day after she got her house, my dog died. He got knocked down and came home limping. Say I said "hi" if you see him his name is Hooch.

I went to the zoo in June with my family because my brother couldn't go on his school trip because he had to go to the dentist. We saw the monkeys first and my brother Cameron said that the monkey had a sore bum and he had to put powder on it. I think the whole zoo had started to laugh. Then we say the seals. There was a big seal swimming around, a baby seal at the side and a medium seal on one of the platforms. The baby seal kept trying to get in the water but medium seal wouldn't let it and every time the medium seal had her back turned the baby seal would pop its head in the water.

I went to the carnival a while back. I went on the Wild Mouse first and that was good. Then I went on Ali Baba, which was all right, and then I went on the Freak Out, which was brilliant. Last year I went on the G-Force but I got sick so I didn't go on it this year. I also played a few games and I won a big teddy bear. But I gave it to my cousin Jordan because after, we got chips and went to my nanny's and Jordan loved it so I let her keep it.

I went on my school trip to the National Aquatic Centre in Blanchardstown. I loved the Black Hole that was brilliant. I also liked the Master Blaster. When our school's name was called we were stuck in the Lazy River (the river that can only go one way) and we had to swim extremely fast to get back to the locker rooms. There was also a swimming pool but I spent all my time on the slides.

I went to Spain in July. It was awesome. When we got off the plane we had to get our bags checked and go through a metal detector. Then a lady named Marie told us we couldn't stay at the hotel we booked and had to stay in an apartment block. The pool was right beside our room. One day we went to a huge water park with millions of slides. I got to hold a Parrott there; I have a picture of it at home. (It has red, green and yellow feathers). We went to a disco another night; there was even a DJ. My friend Elaine and I got up to sing on the Karaoke. We went to a fancy Italian restaurant and I wore my blue Nike dress. We went down to the beach a few days but most of the time we swam in the pool. On the day we were going home I got all my friends numbers and guess what? I left the notebook that I had their numbers in, in the apartment. When I got home I gave my friends their presents and they were delighted with them.

I had a BBQ a while ago because my uncle Martin came home from Australia. My aunt Catherine made punch and Bernadette her sister took a picture of everyone dipping their cups in and drinking it and then since no-one wanted any more she drank the rest out of the bowl. Then she tried to go down the slide, everyone was in hysterics, my aunt had a BQ about a week after, and hers wasn't as fun as ours was.

I went back to school in September and my brother started playschool. He was looking forward to going, all through the summer. But then when he first went in, he started crying and wanted to go home. But now he has lots of friends and likes going. We sang in the church on the 17th September and I went to the 25th anniversary mass. The Arch-bishop De Martin was there.

What do you want to be when you grow up? I'd love to be a architect or a fashion designer because I love to design different clothes and buildings. I even have a special book for drawing them in. Would you like to do a course? I'd absolutely love to do a beautician course, because then I would be able to do my nails and all.

If I had three wishes I would be an actor, live in a mansion, have more wishes, win the lotto and wish my family and I are very healthy. What would you wish for? If I did win the Lotto I'd buy millions of clothes, shoes, a mansion, a swimming pool and a tennis court.

Did you hear they might be putting tax on chewing gum because it costs so much money to take it off the streets? They are also putting pictures of rotted teeth, throats and lungs to discourage people from smoking. I think it's a brilliant idea because when someone goes to take a cigarette they will see that and think twice about smoking.

My aunt went away to a wedding a while ago, so we had to mind my cousins for the weekend. On Saturday we went for a walk down to my aunts to open the curtains and all. My mam was the only one walking because we were all on our bikes. We locked up and all and my mam told Ryan and I to go and check if the community centre was open to get sweets but it wasn't so we went up to Dunnes Stores and got drinks for all of us. Then when we got home I got sick and the next night I stayed up half the night because I was sick so much. The next day I didn't go to school because I was so sick. When my aunt came home she bought us all presents. Dylan and Kyle got Treasure Planet game boy games, Ryan got a Jackie Chan game, Cameron got a set that you make a car with, and if you get bored with it you reassemble it into something else, and I got the best present of all. I got a jumbo set with millions of stuff in it.

My cousin got a tattoo and I think she's way too young, I mean she's only sixteen. She got it on her back because her mother is getting two, one on her shoulder and one on her arm. My mam has a tattoo of a shooting star and my aunt has a tattoo in Chinese writing that's meant to translate into dreams and dreams in Irish means Ashling. My cousin thinks her's is infected because the scab on it looks brown!

I was in the National Children's Choir in the basketball arena. We sang a variety of songs in front of our parents. I was also in the hallelujah concert two years in a row. The first year I done it, Umero Mumba was there and the second year, Declan was there. But they were both brilliant.

Did you see the Spire yet? It's all right, but I think they could have put up something that doesn't look like a lamppost with graffiti on the end of it. I'd say there were much nicer entries. I can see the light at the top of it out my attic window. I could also see some of the fireworks from the opening ceremony of the Special Olympics. I loved them, they were just so beautiful. Do you have TV up in heaven; if you do did you see it?

Did you see hurricane Isabel a few weeks ago. It was a huge hurricane wasn't it? Wasn't it a shame about the war but don't get me wrong I'm glad Sadam Hussein is gone. He was only a dictator. Well that's everything that has happened over the year.

Your friend

Stacey Byrne,
St. Kevin's G.N.S.,
Kilnamanagh,
Tallaght,
Dublin 24.

Dear Grace:

How are you? I suppose you are having a great time in heaven. Did you meet my grandparents Billy and Tim yet? Give them all my love. I watched the Late Late Show on Friday 20th December. I thought your dad was just great and everyone could see he was very sad that you are gone, I know from your picture and your beautiful smile that you were a very special person and that you were and still are very much loved, but your dad knows that you are in heaven. Santa brought me your Dear Grace book for Christmas. I thought it was fantastic and I really enjoyed it especially the bit about Roy Keane and the hurling and football. My granny Peggy is a little better now but she is still very lonely without granddad Tim. It is hard to believe that he is gone over one year now. I miss him a lot as we used to have many great chats about how things were when he was growing up.

Granny Peggy celebrated her birthday on 15th January. My granny Bridie was ninety on the 6th January, we had a huge party in the Waterford Crystal Centre over two hundred people were invited, and of course granny Bridie had to do her party piece. Old King Cole was the poem she said and it went like this.

> Old King Cole was a merry old soul
> A merry old soul was he
> He called for a light
> In the middle of the night
> To go to the W.C.
> The moon shone bright
> On the lavatory door
> And the candle took a fit
> And Old King Cole fell down in the
> Hole
> Up to his eyes
> In s**t

You should have seen her hopping around the place like she was only 21. My mammy says she is cracked, but she really is a laugh. Last year she dressed up as a jockey. You should have seen her with the cap and the whip. She did so much laughing and messing that she nearly wet herself. Unfortunately my granny's house was broken into the following week, everything was thrown around and some presents and money were taken. My granny was devastated.

She is still in shock even now.

My dad was very disappointed in January when the minister for education Noel Dempsey published a list of schools that were going to have new classrooms built. Our school was left out and it wasn't even on the list for future developments.

Some awful things happened around Christmas a priest was struck in Co. Down while he was saying mass. A woman in Manchester went off on holiday and left her eleven-year old son at home to look after himself. Did you know that the new Spire in O'Connell Street, Dublin was made in Dungarvan, Co. Waterford? We are all very proud of this. They started to put it up in place before Christmas but because of the awful weather and high winds they were not able to fit the last piece until the right weather came in mid-January. It was great that Brian Kerr got the job as manager of Ireland. He deserved it. Waterford United won the league of Ireland First Division title, there was great celebrations in Waterford.

In February my dad told me he had a surprise for me. I was so excited later on he told me what the surprise was. I was going to see Manchester United play at the theatre of dreams Old Trafford against their arch rivals Liverpool, I was delighted. Later on that week my mam, dad and I packed our bags and went to Manchester. The next morning I got up bright and early at 9.30am and went into my mam and dads room and shouted "rise and shine" I was so excited I couldn't wait any longer. We left at 12.30pm and we had our lunch first. Man United were playing at 2.30pm. My mother wasn't going to the match, oh no she was going shopping, I don't know what girls like about shopping.

"We'll meet here for our tea at about 5.00pm" she said. A few minutes later we got to old Trafford, the Manchester United Stadium. My dad and I just followed the crowd to get to the stadium. I looked up and saw the gigantic building, I knew this was it. The game kicked off at 3.00pm with a huge roar from both Liverpool and Man Utd Fans. Man United had not beaten Liverpool in years at home but I had a feeling that this was going to be their day. 10 minutes into the game David Beckham the worlds best free taker crossed the ball into the box and Ruud van Nistlerooy scored with a tremendous volley. 20 minutes later Steven Gerrard a Liverpool player was brought down in the box by Rio Ferdinand. The referee blew his whistle and called Ferdinand over and gave him a yellow card and he awarded a penalty.

Michael Owen stepped up, he was going to take the penalty, 'oh no', I thought to myself, suddenly the crowd turned silent. Owen hit the ball, there was a mighty roar as it curled it into the top corner of the net. It was a goal and a good one too. Liverpool were back in it. For the rest of the first half it was quiet and when the referee sounded the half time whistle I'm sure that both teams were happy enough to be going in at a goal apiece. In the second half both teams had a few chances but on the 90 minute mark Ryan Giggs headed in a goal from a David Beckham corner. The final score was 2-1. My dad and I met my mam and we all had a cup of tea and a delicious scone. I said to dad "this day can't get any better". "Oh but it will", he said. You, your mam and me are going to an autograph signing. This day had just got better, an hour later we went to this big hotel umm....... I'm not sure of the hotels name but I know that it was huge. A few minutes later a few of Manchester United's players walked in and started signing autographs I was near the front of the line and I didn't have to wait that long. When it was my turn I had a picture taken with the players, I was amazed that I actually got my picture taken with a few of the Manchester United players, wait until I tell my friends I thought to myself.

All good things have to come to an end unfortunately. When we got back I showed my brother and sisters the autographs, they were amazed. The next day I had a day off from school because I was so tired from the trip, the poor suckers who had to go to school I pity them. When I got into school the next day I showed every one the pictures and the autographs, everyone thought they were great.

On March 11th, we moved into our new house, we like it very much; it has a big garden and lots of grass for me to practise my hurling on. My dad did lots or work painting and decorating with the help of mammy. Aisling had to study very hard for her leaving cert. We all had to be very quiet while she was doing her leaving cert. Conor got a new job and had to buy a new scooter to get in and out of work. Mick McCarthy was appointed Sunderland's new manager I think it is great that he got another chance because I think he did a really good job as Ireland manager. On the 17th of March (you know what that day is don't you - St Patrick's Day) all the family went down to watch the parade, I thought that it was fantastic. Waterford Spraoi was picked as overall winners in the Dublin parade for the best float and design.

On the 3rd of April I made my Confirmation this was a very holy day for me and I had a great time. In April the war in Iraq started between America and Iraq. The United Kingdom was on the side of America. America said that Iraq could have scud missiles hidden and weapons of mass destruction and that they needed to get them and destroy them and that Saddam Hussein had to leave the country. Also Man Utd were Knocked out of the Champions League by Real Madrid over two legs. Although they were knocked out, they put up a good performance and I was proud of them. Getting knocked out of the champion's league wasn't so bad for Man Utd because Arsenal lost to Bolton and left the title in Man Uniteds grasp.

May was quite an eventful month for sports especially for Man Utd. They won the premiership title for the 8th time in eleven years.
Even though Arsenal Lost out on the premiership title they still had some glory by winning the F.A. cup for the second year in row by beating Southampton on a score line of 1-0.
Kilkenny won the National League Final and my Dad was on the line and he said Kilkenny deserved every bit of their glory and should win the All Ireland Final, as well as that, did you know that my Dad went to college with Brian Cody the Kilkenny manager. Speaking about college the 3rd level fees were supposed to be introduced this was bad, as my sister Aisling will be going to college next year when she finishes her leaving cert .My Mother said why did it have to be the same year Aisling was going to college. However Noel Dempsey Minister for Education and Science seemed to find 42 million euro in a hole in his back garden as the week before he had no money and the following week he introduced a 42 million euro package and he said that the 3rd level fees would not be introduced.

Rocky

In July all the family went for a picnic Dad got out the primus stove. Mam cut bread and made sandwiches. Aisling and I got out the cups and saucers Everybody did something. Very soon we were ready for the road. We packed ourselves into our car and drove right across county until we reached the slopes of the Knockmealdown mountains. When we came to a nice green field we decided to go no further. It was a lovely day for a picnic. The sun shone brightly, and the sky was as blue as a hedge-sparrow's egg. Beneath us we could see all of Dungarvan and behind us we could see purple mountains. Mam and Dad sat on a rug and read magazines and the paper Conor, Dean, Aisling and I played soccer .By the time the tea was ready we were like hungry hunters and we certainly ate our fill. Afterwards we played a little more until Dad said that it was time to go home. We gathered up all our rubbish and left everything tidy. Then we packed all our stuff into our car and hit the road. We were all feeling tired and happy after our wonderful day.
In August I played a hurling tournament up in Armagh and we came joint first

In August I played a hurling tournament up in Armagh and we came joint first. I really enjoyed every bit of the trip and I wouldn't miss a chance to go there again. Unfortunately when I got home I found out that my Dog Rocky had been knocked down. I was very sad that he was knocked down and I still am now. Recently I got a new dog and she is a good dog but I will have to train her. At the end or August my Dad and I spent a week camping in a lovely little village called Clogheen in south Tipperary .We visited different places like Mitchelstown caves, Cahir Castle, the Apple Fruit Farm, The Swiss Cottage and we had a game of pool in Ballyporeen in the pub where Ronald Regan the former U .S. President visited.

Well that's about all I have to tell you now. What about you ? I'm in my second week in sixth class now, my sister is in her first year in college and my brother is working, so is my sister Ciara my Mam and my Dad. Ciara is getting married on the 14th of August next year and we're are all busy saving at the moment .I think of you a lot and remember you in my prayers every night.

Please write back soon ,
Your Pal,
Tim O'Byrne,
Fenor N.S., Fenor,
Co. Waterford.

Dear Grace:

My name is Samantha Murphy. My mam's name is Mary Murphy and my dad's name is Sam Murphy. My sister's name is Sonia Murphy, she is a Civil Servant and my brother Kris Murphy is a manager in Dunnes Stores.

I have another member in my family his name is Tom he is my pussycat. In July 2002 we had to go to the vet with Tom because he was coughing up huge hairballs and could not breathe as clearly. The vet we went to is in Fairview across from the hardware shop. When we went into the waiting room we rang the bell and a nurse came out and told us to take a seat and that the doctor would be with us in a minute. After 20 minutes the nurse came back to us and brought us into the examination room where we met Kieran our cat's vet. When he had checked our cat over he told us that Tom had feline asthma. After five minutes he had told us about feline asthma and gave us tablets to help us with his condition and also gave him some injections.

Did you hear about Bertie Ahern's stupid idea? First he wanted a huge jet that was going to cost us millions of euro but eventually he got two smaller jets that are now broken and can't come out of their hangers. Secondly Bertie wanted a sports stadium that the press called the Bertie Bowl. This was also going to cost us millions of euro and he was not allowed to have it constructed (ha ha ha).

Grace, can you see the Spire from up there? In my opinion it's just a huge waste of money. The architect who built it must have been drunk when he was doing the blueprints. I mean it's one hundred and twenty metres tall, three metres wide at the bottom and the very tip is unbelievably small. The crane that was used to build it cost five hundred euro an hour even when it was not in use on the worksite because of rain. It was a big operation and it cost quite a lot. The money that was spent on the Spire should have been spent on homes for the homeless because we need homes for the homeless not a Spire.

Grace, I live in East Wall in Dublin Ireland, I was wondering does it snow in heaven? Because it hardly ever snows in East Wall. Now that I'm talking about what happens in heaven did you happen to see my grans Mary, Kay and Bridie? The reason I have three grans is because my mam's mam Bridie died when she was young and she had a stepmother called Kay. Or perhaps you may have seen my granddads Jimmy or James. Also if there's a bingo club up there say hello to my aunt Biddy for me.

What do you do all day in heaven; can you take holidays or other stuff like that? When I was in London on my holidays I went to Thorpe Park. It was amazing and I wish you could have come too. My favourite ride was Loggers Leap for the first five minutes it seemed peaceful and calm, then we went up a hill and down a hill. This hill was not very high, and then we went on. After another five minutes I thought there was no other hill but then we went up into a dark cave and before I knew it, I was going up and up and up. Then suddenly we came back out into the light. Then we shot down so quickly that the ride was over before it had begun. Can you do stuff like that or play games that you would normally play down here with other children or do you have to play other games like leap cloud and how high can you fly? As well as how you play, how or what do you eat? Is there McDonalds or restaurants or places like that, let me know. Moving on, do you miss anyone or anything from your life here? I know that if I passed on I would miss my mam and dad and my sister and brother and especially my pet cat Tom. Now that I'm talking about pets I think I should tell you my dad races pigeons. I own two of these pigeons, the first pigeon I own is a white called Icy who is a cock pigeon. My second pigeon is a different type of pigeon called a mealy. This means that the pigeon is a particular wheat meal colour. She is a hen pigeon I nicknamed her Amelia. Even though my dad raises the pigeons I give him a lot of help especially in the breeding season, when the pigeons have their young and teach them to fly.

For instance, we have to give the cocks and hens extra food because they have to regurgitate their food to feed their young. When the babies are about three weeks old they can walk and run, which is a bit of a problem for their parents because they're young chase them around for food and they have stopped regurgitating by then. Also to help my dad with the pigeons I do a variety of things. The thing I like doing the most in that variety is watching the youngsters and making sure that their dad's don't get jealous and kill them by pecking them and scratching at them.

That is just one of my many hobbies. My hobbies include swimming, skipping, reading and writing. I would love for football to be one of my hobbies but unfortunately I have asthma and if I were to play football I would have an asthma attack. When I go on holidays I have to bring my inhaler with me.

Speaking of holidays, I went on an airplane for the first time ever in the summer, in England. The experience of being on a plane was not exactly thrilling but different, not bad different, good different. When I was up there it seemed as if we were over all the clouds. Below you could see the white clouds around you and above you, all you could see was blue, but then after a while there was the brightest glow, this was the sun.

As well as going to England I went to my auntie Rose's country cottage in Co. Meath. I stayed for a week and did not want to go home when it was time for me to be picked up. My aunt Rose's country cottage is only one of her houses, her other one is in England. Her country cottage is the only one I've seen. It is a bungalow with five bedrooms, 2 bathrooms, 1 kitchen, 2 parlours and one walk in shower room. When I was there we had a barbeque and every morning we had breakfast on the patio. We went shopping and swimming and we went to her sister's house, my auntie Noleen. Rose's husband is John, he is very nice and he has a cockney accent. John is from England and Rose is from Ireland and still they get on great. I made a very good friend when I was there, his name is Padraig. My other auntie Mary has a grandson who has diabetes. He has to get injections and he has to have his blood sugars tested regularly. If his blood sugar is low he has to eat and if his blood sugar is high he has to exercise. Sometimes when he is in school he has to have his blood sugar tested so his mam has to take him out.

Grace, could I ask you a couple of questions about H.H.T. I don't really know if it's painful or if it affects you when you're alive. When you were in your fathers arms were you scared or were you not aware of what was happening? A lot of times in the news and in the newspapers you hear about people dying and most of the times it makes no impression on you but when I heard about Sept 11th and about all the people who died on the plane and in the Twin Towers it made a big impression on me. A long while after this happened George Bush had reason to believe Saddam Hussein had weapons of destruction hidden in Iraq. Saddam said that he did not have any weapons of mass destruction George would not take no for an answer. The United Nations would not let George go in, but instead sent a team in to search for the weapons. After searching long and hard they came back and told George that there were no weapons of mass destruction in Iraq. But he did not believe the United Nations and decided to go to war anyway. He pleaded with Tony Blair for help and Tony Blair agreed to help him. The world did not approve of this war and there were anti war marches all over the world. I went on an anti was March with my sister Sonia. It was in Dublin and there were thousands of people at it.

I think George Bush made a big mistake and that he should not have gone to war in the first place. It caused a lot of grief for a lot of families, Iraq families and American families alike. George Bush gave his country a bad name but recently we gave our country a good name by hosting the Special Olympics here. The Special Olympics was not only about the people who participated but also about the people who helped. A man called Charlie helped by volunteering his services and chauffeuring people around when it was needed. I think the Special Olympics were fun for the people who participated and also for the people who volunteered. Speaking of fun is it fun in heaven? If I had to choose between staying on earth or going to heaven I would choose to go to heaven, because there are no bills to be paid there as far as I know, and best of all you can't die.

Before I go I have one more thing to tell you, over the summer holidays my dad bought a holiday home. By home I mean mobile home it's in Rush and I will be going there with kettles, mops and the other essentials very soon. I will bring you with me in my mind so you can see it.

I guess for now that's a goodbye.
Samantha Murphy,
St. Columba's N.S., North Strand, Dublin.

Dear Grace:

My name is Eamonn Gaffney. I am ten years old. I heard about this competition in school recently and since then I have been writing this letter.

A surge of sadness shot through me when my teacher told me about you dying at such a young age. It must have been terrible to find out that you had something that would eventually mean your end. I couldn't help wondering how long you were sick before, (I hate saying this, but anyway) before you died. There are lots of things I still wonder about like if you were in much pain or how much medication you had to take, were you sad or were you frightened. Did you think about what Heaven was like or how you were going to get up there through the clouds because you know how many of them there are. I have a sister in heaven, keep an eye out for her. She died when she was a baby but she is twelve now. Make sure to say hello to her if you see her.

I am going to write down a few things about myself so that you will have an idea of what I am like. I live with my Mam, my Dad and my little sister. I have blond hair and green eyes. I was born on the 22nd of December 1992. On my first Christmas, three days after I was born, Santa brought me a cuddly brown bear that growls when you squeeze him. I was only nine months old when I started to walk. Nearly every night after that I used to run straight across my sitting room and bump my head off of the furniture and go to bed with a bump on my head. To get me to bed most nights my Granny or my Mammy used to have to sing me to sleep. When I was one year old I was able to talk. After that I talked and I talked, and I talked, some more. Sometimes I get into trouble in school for talking too much. Another year after that my sister was born. I can remember going up to see her with my Dad, my Granny, my Nannie and my Auntie. When I saw her at first all I can remember was a crying little bundle. My Mam says, when she was looking for us in the hospital nursery, all she had to do was look for the biggest hump because we were big babies.

A while after my sister came home, my Mammy brought us down to a toddlers group on Thursday mornings. In toddlers group I met a lot of the friends that I still have. We had lots of toys to play with there. Some of the things we used to do were paint, make a mess and leave it for the Mams to clean up. My friend Carolanne and I used to go on the seesaw and look at books. Some of the other boys and me used to tear around the hall on little bikes. We used to have great

fun. Them were the good old days!

One year later I started playschool and so did most of my friends from the toddlers group. I can remember one Christmas in playschool, our teacher got us to make a chain of Christmas trees, paint them green and stick sequins and glitter on them. We used them for decorating the classroom. Another day I had the chicken pox. My teacher rang my house and asked my Mam was I going to school. I came up to the sitting room in my green fluffy pyjamas and said, "I don't think so". In playschool I learned my ABC's using Letterland. I also learned how to write and count. I don't think my handwriting has improved that much since then, judging by the snide remarks some of my teachers pass in National School! Some mornings I used to get up late and I had to eat my toast and blackberry jam on the way to school in my Dad's old van, when he was dropping me down. One Christmas I made a paper tree out of an A4 page. I put green paint on my hand and pressed it down on a page a good few times. Then my teacher cut them out and let me stick them on to my tree. Every Christmas my Mam puts it up in a little alcove as a background for our crib. Another Christmas I made a Rudolph face. First I got a paper plate and painted it brown, then I scrunched up little bits of red crepe paper for his nose. My teacher then drew antlers onto paper and cut them out. I painted them yellow and stuck them on. I spent one and a half years in playschool, I really enjoyed it. After I had left playschool my teacher asked my friends Ciaran and Mark and me to come back for one day to visit her. We went and we had a great time.

I started National School in September 1997. Princess Diana was killed in a car accident the day before. On my first day my Mam and Dad took photos of me in my school uniform. My Mam brought me down and left me with all my friends. There wasn't a bother on me because so many of my friends had started there as well. My class was the biggest class in the school; there were sixteen of us. On rainy days we used to play with building straws and plasticine. When I was in first class my sister started in junior infants. I was mean to her in a way, because on her first day I ran on into school and I didn't wait for her. The next year I made my First Holy Communion. I was looking forward to tasting what the Holy Communion was like; it tasted like ice-cream wafers! I felt like a millionaire with my fancy suit and all the money that I got.

I have always been very active and I take part in a wide range of sports. I like tag rugby, hurling, basketball, swimming, Gaelic football, soccer and golf. Overall my two favourite sports are soccer and golf, oops! Fore! Two years ago I started playing soccer for a team. We train Monday and Friday nights and play a match at the weekends. Sometimes we win, sometimes we lose, but that's the way life goes. I'm a Man. United supporter, what about you? If you're a Liverpool supporter don't expect any more letters from me!

I know so little about you. I wish I could see you and talk to you and find out what your hobbies were, what sports you liked or what music you listened to. Sometimes I write poems, ideas just come into my head and I write them down. I have written one for you. Its called "Graceful Grace":

Graceful Grace

I think of you and how you died
Of how you felt or if you cried
Of all your happy times on Earth
And all the love that's in your heart

No more sadness in your life
No more struggles, no more strife
No more worry , grief or pain
No medication or any strain

No more trouble up above
Floating heavenly like a dove
Through fluffy clouds as white as snow
Drifting lightly as you go

Some things on Earth are not good
And everything's bad down in Hell
The most important thing is that
You're in Heaven now safe and well

I hope that you're happy in Heaven
I hope that you are at peace
I hope you have lots of friends there
And may your happiness never cease

I hope you like my poem. I tried my best to write it so that you and your parents would enjoy reading it. I sometimes think about how much your family must miss you. They must have really felt sad when the doctors told them that you had what you had. If I had your parents' address I would post my poem to them and hope that they would read it. What were your parents' names, what was your surname, did you have any brothers or sisters, what ages are they? Other things I would like to know are if your parents have written a book about your life story , if they did what is its' title and where can it be bought? What is your date of birth, where did you live, did you live in the countryside or a town? Does your house have a garden? Did you have any pets? If there is a book about you I would probably find all the answers to questions in it, but I haven't found one so far so they won't be answered yet.

I have just moved into fifth class. A lot of things happened this year. My sister made her First Holy Communion in May; it's not fair she got more money than I did! Around that time I got sick. I was in hospital but I was allowed out for a few hours to go to my sister's Communion. When I found out what was wrong with me one of the first things I asked my Mam was, "would I die from it". It was a frightening experience but I felt better when my Mam said that it would not kill me. I was very sad right around then but it was nothing compared to what you must have been. As it turned out my treatment wasn't as bad as I thought; yours must have been dreadful. I do have to watch what I eat now. Isn't it all a pain?

The next time I write to you maybe I will know a lot more about what you were like, then I will be able to keep you up to date on all of your interests. I will also let you know what is happening down here, I'm sure much more exciting things are happening up with you! I'll always be glad that I heard about you, maybe you will be able to visit me in my dreams and we can have a good old chat. Do you think you could manage that? Take care, I'll be in touch.

Your new friend.
Eamonn Gaffney,
Barndarrig N.S.,
Wicklow.

Dear Grace:

Hi it's Conor Browne again, In case you don't remember I live in Co. Waterford and I'm eleven years old. I am writing to tell you what has happened to me and also about some worldwide events over the past year. I hope you learn something new out of my letter.

I'll start by telling you about the war in Iraq. Basically the president of America (President Bush) and the Prime Minister of the United Kingdom (Tony Blair) went to war with Iraq earlier this year. They say that they were going in for the good of the people of Iraq but I don't think this is true. I think they were going in to get oil (There's a lot of oil in Iraq). They may be doing a little bit of good there, but I don't think they are doing much good because many people have died in Iraq since they've gone in. In my opinion I think President Bush and Tony Blair are very mean and ruthless people.

Changing the subject, earlier this month the anniversary of the September 11th attack took place, which is now known a the "9/11." If you don't know what happened on the 11th of September two years ago it was when two planes crashed into the Twin Towers. This very cruel thing was done by a group of terrorists called "Al Queda." They were settled in Afghanistan. That day my two cousins should have gone and been there when the planes crashed into the Twin Towers, but they stayed in their hotel because their mother was going over to America to see them. Thank God they didn't go.

At the start of the year we got a new teacher called Mrs Newell. She is very nice and she loves Irish. She teaches fifth and sixth class. I am in sixth class. Every Friday she gives us a test in Irish, spellings, geography, history and maths.

On to a different subject, my aunt and uncle came over from England to see us. They also came over to mind the house and the dog while we were on holidays. Their names are Ronnie and Jean. They are very nice and kind. They came over near the start of the summer holidays. They live in Newcastle in England. I really like it when they come to our house.

Earlier this year the Waterford Under 21 Gaelic team won the Munster Finals. This was great news while it lasted but sadly the hurling team got knocked out in the All Ireland Semi-Final. My favourite players on the team are, Tony

Browne and John Milan. In case you are wondering I am not related to Tony Browne. I just hope that our local club Gaultier can do well because we are playing in the final sometime soon. We are playing St. Saviours. We have already played the final but we have to play it again because we drew the first time. We should have won except the referee took their side and played an extra seven minutes that should not have been there. During that time they came level with us. I think the referee was very unfair in that match and I hope we have a different referee for the re-match. I also hope we beat St. Saviours this time.

At the start of August this year, my family and I went on our holidays to France. We had booked a small house inland, in Cognac. On the way there we got stuck in a thirty-three kilometres long traffic jam. Overall it took us two days travelling down to Cognac. We were staying in a place called "Madam Lascaux." This place had a few small houses together. It had a nice swimming pool with a springboard and a small slide. The place where we were staying was in a vineyard. When I was there I bought my mother two bottles of Rose and bought two bottles of Pinot for my dad to thank them for bringing me on holidays.

It also had a games room, with a pool table, table football, target practice (Using flat circles of wood and trying to hit them into archways with something like a cue) and table tennis and a play area with swings and special climbing walls.

When we were there fifteen thousand people died because it was too hot but we did not know this until we were actually there. Some days it was over one hundred degrees and we couldn't buy a fan because all the hospitals had them. It was a weird sensation to walk to the door or to the window and feel hot air blow into your face.

While we were there I met a boy called Pierre (Peter) and a girl called Lucy. I made good friends with them and we played pool together and went swimming together.

On the way home it took us two days to get to Cherbourg. When we were on the ferry my brothers and I met a boy called Owen. He was fifteen years old. I got his email address and I am hoping to send him a message. When we arrived in Rosslare we had a short drive home to Dunmore East. I really enjoyed our time in France and I cannot wait until next year.

Earlier on this year my granny Mary and her friend Peggy came to visit us. They both live in Co. Down in Northern Ireland. They stayed for about two to three weeks. They both are really kind and funny. When they were here my mom, granny, Peggy and me went to the Hook Lighthouse and got a tour of it. I really enjoyed their stay. And I hope they come down again soon.

A good while after that my granny Mary and two cousins Dezzie and May came down to visit us. Dezzie and May live in Canada. They are very kind and thoughtful. Their son, my cousin is the mayor of a town in Canada. This town is called Sarnia. He is in a documentary. I think it is about guns and how there are more guns in Canada and less in America but more people get shot and killed in America than in Canada. I think the film is called "Bowling for Columbine." In it he is called "The Voice of Reason." He is very nice and is engaged.

Quite a while ago the Sars disease broke out around the world. This killed a good few people. It was a very sad time for many people. I am glad it did not kill anyone I know, but it could just as well have because I know a lot of people who work in the hospital or were in there at the time of this break out

Anyway on to a different subject, did you hear about Ireland's new football manager Brian Kerr? In case you did not know Ireland's old manager was Mick McCarthy. I think they are both good managers but I think Brian Kerr is better. My favourite player on the team is John O'Shea because he's a very good player and he was born in Ferrybank that lies just across the river from Waterford.

Earlier this year the man who is said to be the world's most famous country singer, died. His name was Johnny Cash. He was from America. This man had a lot of talent. I think country music is ok but I prefer Irish music and classical music.

Back to sports, Kilkenny won the double double; this means that the seniors and the minors won the All Ireland Final in hurling two years in a row. The seniors were playing Cork in the final. I was going for Kilkenny. I would have gone for Cork because Kilkenny had won it the year before and they were the favourites except that Cork beat Waterford senior team and then we had to go through the back door if we wanted to win the All Ireland final which made it a lot harder for us to get there.

A little while ago there was a hurricane in America. It hit the Carolina's. The hurricane was named Isabel. It killed about three or four people. A lot of people were lucky to escape alive. The hurricane reached Washington D.C. but by then it had lost all it's strength and was only like a rainstorm. But before the hurricane reached Washington D.C. President Bush had left in case he got hurt.

A little while ago there was a program on television called "Cabin Fever." On this programme a good few people were picked out randomly and were put on a boat. And every week somebody was voted off. Who ever won got one hundred thousand euro. Elaine the manager of our local Centra was on the program. After a few weeks into the program the boat crashed. It took a while for them to get a new boat that looked the same as the old one, but they did and from then on the program was called "Cabin Fever Two". I was hoping she would win and she did! I think she deserved to win not just because I know her but also because she acted like herself on the program. She was donating some of the hundred thousand euro to the charity shop, her mom works in (The I.S.P.C.A.) and she was holding a big party for the people of Dunmore. I don't think you could have picked a better person to win the show than Elaine.

Earlier on this year the Special Olympics was held in Dublin in Lansdowne Road. It was great fun to watch on television. It was very nice watching the introduction to the whole thing. It had loads of music and dancing which was great but I will never forget the River dance. This was just brilliant with all the Irish dancers and the great musicians. I know the fellow who was playing the uilleann pipes in that song. My dad is a good friend with him. I think the Special Olympics is a great idea and I can't wait till the next time it's on.

During the summer the Bluegrass Festival was held in our village (Dunmore East). It's on every year and I really enjoy it. It's great fun going around to all the different pubs to listen to the different bands. I really enjoyed it and can't wait until next year to go to it again.

Grace, I've really enjoyed writing to you and I hope you learned something. I hope you enjoyed it as much as I did because it helped me remember a lot of stuff that I had forgotten. I can't wait to write to you again. Please write back.

Your friend forever,
Conor Browne,
Killea Boys N.S., Waterford.

Dear Grace:

I hope you are enjoying heaven. Another year has passed and many positive and negative events have happened on this planet. I wish I could just impart positive events to you, but as usual, life is not a bed of roses!

As you know speed is a problem on Irish roads. It sometimes frightens me, when I hear about people being killed in car crashes. I was delighted, when the Minister for Transport, Seamus Brennan, introduced penalty points. It took me a while to understand penalty points, but I eventually learned. Now I see my Mum slowing down when she comes to speed limits. Twelve points means she will lose her licence. You can get penalty points for speeding, not wearing a belt and going through red traffic lights etc. Since the penalty point system was introduced, in November, the amount of accidents on Irish roads have decreased. Funnily enough, Seamus Brennan just passed his driving test!

In March 2003, the government hired builders to erect a sliver metal pole, with spikes on top, which looks like the crown of thorns Jesus was told to wear. They called this weird pole 'The Spike'. It is found in O'Connell's Street in Dublin. My Mum and Dad brought me in to see it and I thought it was a dreadful emblem for Ireland, considering the emblem for Paris is the Eiffel Tower and Dublin's emblem is a pole. Even the clogs and tulips, the emblems of Amsterdam are far better than Dublin's emblem. The emblem of Paris fascinated me, as you could go to the top if it, drink tea and coffee on it and see all of the sights of Paris there. As usual, my Mum was suffering from vertigo, but the higher the better for me! (The 'Spike' was supposed to be built in two thousand to celebrate the millennium. However, like the buses, it was late arriving!

We have had a mini heat wave in Ireland this year. We had the warmest weather in April. Many people say we had the hottest April and summer, that we have had in forty-four years. This, in my opinion is an amazing record for Ireland! We were very lucky but over in Toronto and China, things weren't so good!

In Toronto and China, a disease called S.A.R.S. spread and many people died as hospitals became over-crowded. S.A.R.S. was a very contagious flu-like disease, which killed most people who caught the disease. S.A.R.S. stands for: Severe Acute Respiratory Syndrome. There were many meetings with the

government, whether Special Olympic athletes from S.A.R.S. affected countries should be allowed to take part in the Special Olympics. The answer was no! Nobody wanted an out-break of S.A.R.S. in Ireland.

The Special Olympics was a huge event, especially as Ireland hosted them! There were many sports such as: gymnastics, horse riding, swimming, golf, bowling, cycling, running, tennis and football.

My cousin Jack, who I have always admired, as he has special needs, took part in the gymnastics in June 2002 and got through to the Special Olympics 2003. My Godmother was given nine tickets for the opening ceremony and I was fortunate enough to be given one of them. My Granny came to Dublin and stayed with us, as did my Grandad, as they were also invited to the opening ceremony. At the opening ceremony Mary McAleese made a speech and she wore a beautiful baby-blue dress and jacket. Also the Corrs, Samantha Mumba, U2 and Ronan Keating sang. Mary Davies also made a charming speech to the Athletes! Arnold Swarzenegger and Roy Keane made special appearances! Rita Connolly and Ronan Tynan sang a song, which was written for the Special Olympics called: May we Never have to Say Good Bye! It was beautiful! My cousin Jack was taking part in the gymnastics, this meant that his performance was in the R.D.S. on the 26th June at 12.45. I had the day off school YIPPEE!! My family and I got the train to Sandymount and walked to the R.D.S. It was packed! Everywhere you looked you saw green and yellow tracksuits. I saw my cousin, also dressed in green and yellow. He looked great! I also saw a few of his friends: Tara, Ciara and Orlaith (from the Irish team). Jack was with his coach, Dermot and they were doing a weird handshake, which you see most boys doing! Jack did his performances. He did the pommel horse, which meant you had to do gymnastics on a thick line, held up by brown sturdy wooden sticks. (I admit, I wouldn't be able to do it). He also did the horizontal bars, the rings, the vault and a floor routine. In my opinion he was excellent! Before and after each of these performances Jack had to salute the judge. The next day, at twelve noon, my Mum collected us from school (on our last day WO-HOO!) and off we went, back to the R.D.S. to see the results of the gymnastics. Every time a winner came out on stage, they had a beautiful sunflower, which they threw. Unfortunately, I didn't catch any. Anyway Jack won a gold medal for the pommel horse, a silver medal for the rings and a bronze medal for the horizontal bars and five ribbons. He did excellent work!

The closing ceremony was amazing! The famous people this time included Bertie Ahern (BOO!), Blue, Busted, Liberty X and Westlife. Another great late night for me. It was like being at a concert. I think that now, because of my cousin, Jack Connolly, I will never be afraid of people with special needs and I will always understand him! Also it is great having a cousin who is famous, but, we need to find a cure for his swelled head!

In the aftermath of the attack on the Twin Towers in New York, America turned the attention of the war, on terror to Iraq. George Bush ordered Saddam Hussein to get rid of Iraq's nuclear weapons and chemical weapons. In April, America and Britain invaded Iraq. Saddam Hussein's government were overthrown. Now the attention is focused on rebuilding Iraq giving it a proper government chosen by its people. Where does Saddam Hussein keep his c.d.'s? In a rack (Iraq).

Enough about the current affair topics. My social life has gone down hill from Monday to Thursday lately as I am back to school. However I have brilliant memories of the summer. Especially in May when my teacher, Ms O'Sullivan took my class and I, to Blessington for our school tour. We were able use a real bow and arrow. It was like being in Robin Hood! Also we were allowed to do wall climbing. You had to wear a leather object which looked like a nappy and you were tied to many strings and ropes. It was amazing! Also, we did orienteering which is just a fancy name for a treasure hunt or walking. My group did a treasure hunt. My friend Sarah and I did it together and we came third last. The best activities we did were canoeing and kayaking. The kayaks were the best. My group and I aimed to break the record of twelve people fitting into a canoe and we succeeded. We got thirteen people into the canoe. Suddenly, the boat toppled over! It was hilarious, in my opinion, but it wasn't so good for others!

In my class there is a girl called Sarah Fennell and she was born on the 17/09/92 and so was I. We were also born at nine thirty a.m. in Irish time but unfortunately she was born in Holland, which is an hour behind us. This means she was born at eight thirty a.m. Anyway, in June, we were planning our parties and we both wanted to do the same things go to the cinema and pizza hut. So then we decided to have a double party. I thought this was a great idea! We needed to decide on a day which suited both of us. The only day that suited both of us was Friday 13th bad luck day! We booked the cinema and Pizza Hut for twenty-three people. Sarah came to my house to do the invitations, and then, for the first time, the computer broke down! Typical! We had to wait one hour and eventually we got the invitations done. We were going to see 'Dumb and Dumber'. Other than the making of the invitations the party went great! The film was also very good! Never have your party on

Friday 13th and if you do, beware of the bad luck!

Also, in June 2003, a girl in my class called Avril, was able to get my class and I an invitation to go to the Dail, as her aunty works there. We were given a tour around and we were allowed to watch a small argument. All of the paintings and walls were painted with detail. As we were going into the Dail we met Charlie Bird and we took a picture. Although, in one picture, Charlie looks like he is drunk!

Just before I go you will be glad to know that in the past year, that the "Dear Grace" project has helped raise awareness of your illness. Hopefully, the money raised, will help fund treatment for the disease, then your death will not have been in vain. I'm going out to play now because the weather is sunny and warm. It might be years from now, before we have weather this nice again! What is seldom is wonderful! or as they say 'mar a deirtear!'

Your friend,
Hannah Timmins,
St. Patrick's Girls N.S.,
Donabate, Co. Dublin.

Dear Grace:

How are you? I have missed you since you passed on and I hope you still feel the joy that you felt here on earth. In case you're wondering this is Sally, your Springer Spaniel. Oh how I wish that you were more than a memory and that you were with me still, to comfort me in my sorrow.

I have grown quite ragged in your absence, too many late nights howling woefully at the ever-bright moon. The family's moods have ranged from sometimes a forced happiness to shameless woe at other times. At first I was totally ignored, which suited my own mood, but not those of my stomach. I clawed at the food press for over an hour before your father fed me. After a few days the rejection changed to leniency, constant brushing and a plentiful supply of food and water, not to mention tid-bits whenever I whined or begged.

I was confused at the sorrowful air around the house and constant trips to different places we used to go, made in a futile effort to find you. My hopes rose again when the school year started. Every day for at least a week I would race to the door and yelp and chase my tail in breathless anticipation of hearing the familiar sound of weary feet trudging to the door. But every day I walked back with my tail between my legs and my heart feeling it had a rend down it's centre. I finally accepted the inevitable that you were lost to me, to us all. At first I felt a rage. How dare you leave without saying goodbye were my initial thoughts, but the fury passed quickly and was replaced by a deep sorrow that nestled its way to the core of my being.

To add to my misery my best friend Zeek died as well. We were out one day running happily on the road when a car sped around the corner and blew Zeek fully off his feet into the air. He landed at an impossible angle next to me and I heard the loud snap of breaking bones. The driver hadn't even stopped. The loss of Zeek was a small consequence compared to you.

Lonely weeks past, swept away by the harsh winter winds, the turmoil's on pregnancy played on me as they do every mother. I was one month into pregnancy. Your father was my saviour over those few weeks, with the exception of one day, when every ones mind was dull and few words were uttered under our roof at least. I think the date was 11th of September. Only days after four little miracles were born. Four hairless beauties. (I'm sure they looked ugly to others but to me they will always be wonderful). Worn out after the birth, I could only lie exhausted but happy on the rough garage floor. While four tiny wonders squeaked desperately for milk. I rolled wearily over to show them my underbelly. They groped clumsily around for a few seconds before finding their target. After a few minutes their tiny stomachs were full, so they nestled closer for warmth and fell into a deep sleep. The next day the rest of the family were overjoyed to find little balls of joy in their garage. Water and food were brought out for me; I wolfed the food and lapped gratefully at the water. The pups began to squeak again so I complied again for another few minutes before they all fell into a deep sleep. Over the next two days the cycle of eating, feeding, providing warmth and sleeping continued until on one glorious morning as the sun chased the moon out of the sky and shone its first beams through the singular glass window to shed its warmth on me and my pups, and through that light I saw the tiny eyelids easing upwards and even smaller eyes began to take in their surroundings. They took a few steps gingerly at first but then growing more confident began to explore. Nothing within their reach escaped a good sniffing. It was tiring work for them so it wasn't long before all four pups were back for food and as always after eating they feel asleep. I looked joyously at my slumbering pups, I nearly barked in joy I was so proud of them, my little pups, and their hair had grown as well. Now all four had a sleek coat of fur. When the family strode in for their morning visit, they found to their delight the pups roaming around the garage. The pups froze, frightened of the huge humans gawking at them, I walked up behind the lead pup and prompted him forward with my nose, growing bold from my presence, and he took a few cautious steps towards your father and nervously sniffed his leg up and down. Satisfied he turned away.

The other pups all took their turn at this. Your father beckoned me out into the dazzling sunlight, I paced excitedly out, I had been in the garage for a week. My pups in a line behind me. A gust of wind swept gently across my face and suddenly, I felt very energetic, I bounded around the garden taking in all the familiar scents and sounds. I turned around to see if my pups were following me, and there they were, half running, half stumbling across the garden. Your dad had gone away, so I decided to use my time outside to teach the pups. They absorbed everything I had to say and I promised to test them at the end of the week.

They played comically for the rest of our time. This was repeated for every day for a few weeks, and my most painful memories of you were diminished. The pups grew steadily over the next few weeks and various people came to speak with your parents and study the now stronger sleeker pups though as all pups do, they retained their comical behaviour.

The first pup was a strong girl with blue eyes, soft jet-black fur, and an ever-wagging tail and her name was Max. The second was more cautious it had deep hazel eyes and fuzzy fur with black and brown spots all over its body, and a shade light brown on its head. The last pup was also a female and had a gentle white fur all over her body, with the exception of its tail, which was jet black. It turned into everything it was told and wasn't quick to act but did act when she thought it was right. The first pups name was Max. The second's was Fido and the third was Grace. Then one day a couple with a chubby child entered the garage. When the family saw the pups they immediately picked them up. The meekly protesting pups were handed over, some money was exchanged and they left. I stood there transfixed in a newly felt sorrow, my babies gone, lost to me as you are.

I remained in this sullen state for weeks not even Christmas cheered me up, I moped sadly around the house and garden and then one sunny morning in early January the family woke me up and sat me in the car. In about five minutes we reached our destination, we got up and strode quickly to the door. A shrill doorbell rang cutting through the crisp morning air. The woman that had come on that terrible day, when my pups had been stolen from me, led me out into a huge garden where beautiful snowdrops littered the fresh earth and a towering oak tree was laid bare to the harsh winds of Ireland. Plants of all sorts lay hoarded at the back but most beautiful of all were three dogs in the middle of the garden. I shrieked across the garden yelping in delight, my babies! Grace saw me first and joy shone in her eyes as she bounded towards me in a few seconds we were all together rolling and playing joyously. All traces of my sorrow were forgotten. Much too soon, your father dragged me inside and sat me in the car.

Next morning, barking next door woke me up (the house next door had been vacant for some time) I rushed out instinctively and began to bark back at the new intruder. I slipped into the garden by my own special way to be met by a fluffy blue eyed most handsome West Highland white terrier. He was eyeing me up but you know my taste in dogs, tall dark and handsome. I ran at him and butted him playfully so as not to give him the wrong idea. He cuffed me across the right ear for that, and soon we were both running around joyously playing our hearts out in a playful fight. I said my goodbyes and returned home to collapse into bed. I made a pleasant excursion into his garden every day after that. I found out that he had lost his master, and soon we became great friends.

Anyway that's my year, hope you had an excellent year. Don't forget to look for Zeek up there, in your next letter please fill me in on the meaning of life.

Love
Sally.

Olan Kelleher,
Goggins Hill N.S.,
Ballinhassig,
Co. Cork.

Dear Grace:

I'm really excited about writing to you at long last! So much has happened since you've been gone, not only to me but to so many people all over the world. Some things were good but unfortunately, some of them were very bad. I'm only going to tell you about some of the things that I think you would be really interested in……..

For over five months now there has been a dreadful war in Iraq. America and Britain have sent soldiers to Iraq from all of their military bases. They are exploding bombs, invading cities and all of the Iraqis are very frightened and upset. Hundreds of thousands of people's lives have been traumatised because of this war. The whole world has watched this happening and everyone is in complete shock because of it. I don't agree with it at all though. I think it's very unfair that so many people have been hurt so badly by it.

Anyway, let's talk to you about something on a lighter note! I'm pretty sure you remember the band called Westlife. They've released some huge hits recently. My favourite song that they released is, "Flying Without Wings." A great band called S Club 7 has split up this year. I'm not sure if you heard of them. They had three boys and four girls, all great dancers and very talented singers. I went to see them in a concert in the Point in Dublin last year. I got the tickets as a Christmas present. Their first big hit was "Reach for the Stars." Everybody liked dancing to it, especially my mother! You should see her when it comes on the TV or Radio. I hide!

Remember mobile phones? They used to be big, heavy and awkward. They never fit into pockets. Well, you should see them now! 1 My phone is only four inches long and one inch wide! And, some of the latest models can actually take photos and play videos!! My phone has a colour screen and a radio! Texting is the thing these days and there is nearly a new language called "Txt." An example of a text message is: "Heya, How r u? Wat ya at?" Words are shortened like that for speed in texting. (And to make sure that your parents don't have a clue what we're talking about).

Now, onto every girl's favourite subject, fashion! I am officially obsessed with clothes! You should see my wardrobe! Really though, I love clothes. Fashion is my passion and so on!! Some of my favourite shops are, (get ready) Boston, Pull and Bear, Claire's Accessories, Miss Selfridges and Showco.

I like a lot of different styles actually. I'm sure you'd love some of the styles that are out now, such as mini skirts and clothes that were out in the 1950's. I really like the old fashion clothes.

I don't think you would have heard about David Blaine. Well, trust me there is a lot to tell (in case you haven't guessed, I think he is gorgeous)!! You see, David Blaine is a sort of magician but not the type of magician who pulls rabbits out of hats or does TV shows with all the strings or the beautiful assistants. He just stops people on the streets of Manhattan or Chicago and will do an absolutely astonishing trick. For instance, he once picked up a dead fly off the ground and put it into a mans hand and brought it back to life! Is that amazing or what? Well apart from being a magician, he also does things that are absolutely unbelievable.

Some of the things he's done are: He stood on a pole in the centre of Central Park in New York for eighty-three hours. He buried himself alive for seven days surviving on only water. He stood inside a sculptured block of ice for sixty-two hours, amazing man! But if you thought they are amazing, listen to this. He is now attempting to stay in a glass box with no food, just water, for forty-four days! The box is hanging over the river Thames in London and people spend hours looking at him doing absolutely nothing. Amazing or what? It's a big bonus that he is really good looking too!!!

There have been so many movie releases lately that it's hard to just pick out a few! A lot of sequels came out but I never got a chance to see any of them. I think my favourite film this year would have to have been A Walk to Remember. It's a really sad story about a girl who was sick with Cancer. Sometimes when I see what happens to other people I think about how lucky I am to be happy and healthy. My favourite film that came out over the summer is Two Weeks Notice. It stars Hugh Grant and Sandra Bullock and it's a hilarious romantic comedy. I'm sure you'd love it!

What everyone is talking about this year are celebrities. So much has happened! Well, if you remember the boy band NSync, then you'll remember Justin Timberlake! He is THE guy of the year this year. He broke up with Britney Spears, had number one singles in the United States and is now dating Cameron Diaz. Meanwhile, Britney is dating Cameron's ex!! David Beckham has signed with Real Madrid! It's true, David, Victoria and their two sons have moved to Spain. We could be here for days if I told you all that has happened in the celeb world so I think I'll leave it at that for now!

I'm sure you can remember some of the TV programmes that were on when you were here. Well, they're all still on but there are loads more! Do you remember Friends? Well, they're in their tenth and last series. Can you believe it? Rachel has had a baby and Monica and Chandler got married!

Also, new, and really successful shows are reality TV shows. There are shows that show people doing their jobs or how they go about their life. I'll give you an example of one of them. Big Brother, for instance, is a show that puts twelve housemates in a house for ten weeks. While they are there they have to complete tasks so they can pay for food. Also, they have to nominate people every week to be up for eviction.

When they are nominated, the public then, wait for it, TXT in their votes on their mobile phones for who they want to see getting evicted and the one that gets the most votes has to leave the house. Another show is Pop Idol. I will tell you more about that in the next letter. You can guess what it's about by the name.

Oh, Grace, I have to tell you about this totally unbelievable looking guy!! He's completely DDG drop dead gorgeous!! It's Prince William! He's six foot tall, blonde haired, blue eyed, a real boy-next-door look!! He was 21 this year and, of course, went all out for his birthday. And as usual, it made front page! One of the things that happened was when a man dressed up as Osama Bin Laden went and tried to destroy the party! There have been a lot of stories about Prince William in the papers recently but he's ignored them all, which I think is a very good thing to do. Until he hears from me!

Do you have a favourite book? I don't, I have hundreds!! In case you couldn't guess, I love books! I am a complete fanatic!! Loads of books have come out recently. I haven't read all of them but I read a lot of them. Two of my favourite books are "Little Women" and "My Funny Valentine." The book I'm reading right now is called "David Blaine Mysterious Stranger" which I am enjoying. It is about David Blaine (obviously!) and it tells you all about the stunts that he's done, which is really interesting. The types of books I like are romantic, horror and romantic comedies!

Okay let's talk about everybody's favourite things! Holidays! I had a brilliant holiday this year! We went to Costa del Sol in Spain, which was absolutely fab. The weather was great and then, in Ireland we had the nicest summer we've had since 1995 and I still didn't get a tan! Mam keeps me plastered in factor 60 sun tan lotion. I would have a better chance of a suntan lying under a light bulb. I met loads of new friends in Spain and had a great time with them. I love Spain. It's where I almost always go on holidays and I've always liked it there.

I'm in sixth class now and I have to say that it is really shocking that it's happened so fast. My sister has just started school this year and it's really strange to look at her and think of when I was her age. Last year, our school won the Green Flag. I was on the committee that received the flag at a special ceremony. Some of the girls in my class did very well in football last year. They won loads of matches. Our town basketball team recently won the third best in Ireland at the National Community games. That was an incredible achievement.

It's a bit sad that it's my last year in this school and that I have to say goodbye to some of my friends at the end of the year, but we're friends since we started school together and nothing will ever change that.

It's autumn now and Halloween is approaching which is great. I've always loved Halloween and anything to do with horror so this year is no exception! Trick or Treat, sweets, scary films, are my idea of a perfect night in.

Then next, it's Christmas time. My favourite time of year. Presents, lazy days inside, blazing fires and Christmas Carols. I've already got my present list ready but I won't tell you about that because if I do we'll be here until Christmas! But I don't really mind what I get for Christmas because to me it's a time to spend with people you love.

Well Grace, it's nearly time for me to go. When I started writing I wasn't sure what to write to you about and now its strange, I'm having difficulty saying goodbye to you. I really hope you enjoyed hearing all my news. I would give anything to know what you think of everything that's happened this year, I hope you are happy and I will write to you soon and tell you about anything else I have found out.

Loads a' love
Lesley Kehoe xoxoxoxo
Scoil Eimhín Naofa, Monasterevan, Co. Kildare.

P.S.   I looked up the word Grace in the dictionary. The definition of Grace is "a state of being pleasing of God." I had no doubt that you always will be.

THE MANY FACES OF SADDAM HUSSEIN.

Dear Grace:

I have often heard it said that 'life must go on', and I hope your family realise this and that time is a great healer for them. It must have been very hard for them watching you suffer. I am sure you are happy now and that all your sufferings are over, so that is one small consolation to them. If you had been a lot older when you died, the tragedy would not have been such a shock to so many people. People refer to life as the four seasons, but you left in the springtime of your life. You never experienced the joys of spring. Your sufferings took all that away. However, many will miss you and must carry this burden. We must all try to share your family's loss. Many will miss your gentle soul. I have often wondered what it's like up where you are now. I know everything's perfect there. I'm sure you're really happy. By the way, could you just say hello to my relatives for me. Tell them I miss them. I wonder if you can play football up there. But I suppose I'll find out when I die. When I die, I hope to see you. I would like to know you a bit better. I hope we'll be the best of friends. Apart from the changes your death has left, there are many, many other changes that happened since you died, some of which I will tell you now.

On the 11th September 2001 in America, suicide bombers crashed three planes. Two planes crashed into the Twin Towers in New York and one into the Pentagon. It was just after 9.00 a.m. in New York on a working day and most people were just arriving in the busy Twin Tower Buildings for their day's work. There was chaos all around. People were screaming and panicking. A lot of people were trapped on the top floor where the airplanes had crashed. People were absolutely terrified. They were so afraid that many, many people jumped out of the windows. Some people jumped out windows on the 80th floor. The huge Towers collapsed and almost 3,000 people were killed and thousands were injured. Some of the bodies were never found because they were completely burnt in the fire. Osama Bin Laden was the main suspect for the crashes. It was heart-breaking watching families mourn their loved ones, on the television. They even played tape recordings of last minute conversations of people's last minute phone calls to their loved ones.

Do you know I think the whole world hasn't been the same since this horrific act of terrorism. People, especially Americans, seem to be terrified about things they were never afraid of before. The result is that all over the world security has been stepped up everywhere especially in airports and public places. George Bush, President of the United States of America promised the

American people that those responsible for this horrific act of terrorism, would be brought to justice. He therefore declared war on the Talabans in Afghanistan because these were Bin Laden's followers. Many suspects were captured and are still held in Guantanamo Bay and these may face the death penalty yet. Unfortunately, many innocent people were killed during this war but Bin Laden was never captured. We do know that he is still alive and hiding away somewhere in the mountains because he sends tapes of himself to the Americans to prove this. As he is still alive, people continue to be afraid of more acts of terrorism like the Twin Towers tragedy.

Then this year on the 18th March 2003, war loving George Bush declared war again, but this time on Saddam Hussein, the ruler and king of Iraq. He did this because he said they were making nuclear and biological weapons there and they were afraid that he may use these on the rest of the world. We don't know if they really had these weapons at all because nobody found any trace of them. This war was sad because many American and British soldiers were killed as well as many Iraqi soldiers and innocent Iraqi people. The war was shown live on the television and it was unbelievable to see people being shot at and others being killed. We saw the air raids going on day and night. As the airplanes dropped thousands of bombs, destroying buildings and houses, the whole area lit up. It was very hard to believe and understand that people were being killed at that very minute while we were watching them doing this, on television.

Now although the war is long over, the situation in Iraq is very bad. The country is in a bad state and the Americans are trying to get the United Nations to help get the country back to normal. I don't know how long, but it will probably take many years to rebuild the country again. People say George Bush just wanted to go to war because of Iraq's wealthy oil wells. I suppose we will never hear the full story. Anyway, Saddam Hussein was never captured or killed. He managed to escape. His loyal army helped to hide him and nobody knows where he is now, but the Americans are still hunting him down. They have a list of 50 wanted Iraqis, and they want them dead or alive. They would prefer to have them alive to find out more about Saddam and where he is. They have captured or killed a lot of these 50 people. Many of these were friends and cousins of Saddam, but two of them were Saddam's sons. The television even showed their dead bodies. The Americans said they had to show the bodies of the two sons, because if they didn't the Iraqi people would not believe that they were dead. Saddam and his two sons seemed to have been awful bad men. They loved torturing and killing millions of Iraqi men, women and children. It just seems like the Iraqi people were terrified of them because if they disobeyed them in any way, they would kill them. I guess that was one good thing about the war - all that is stopped now. The Iraqi people are safe now from Saddam and his family and followers.

Anyway Grace, that's most of the bad news around the world since you left it. Some good news is the Millennium celebrations, which started in 1999, probably before you left, went on into 2001. It lasted a long time. We celebrated and celebrated and celebrated and it was great to see everybody enjoying themselves and in great form all the time.

You will never guess Grace, what I came across yesterday. I decided to surf the web to see if I could find anything on HHT the illness you died from and I got loads of information on it. Guess what I found? A photograph of you in your Holy Communion dress with your sister. I couldn't believe my eyes. It has made me feel so much closer to you now that I know what you look like. Your Holy Communion dress is lovely, it is very like the one I had for mine. Your tiara and veil are lovely too. My Granny made me a carrick-macross lace veil for my Holy Communion and I'm going to keep it for my daughter's Holy Communion (if I ever have a daughter!). You look really pretty and you have lovely blonde hair in the photograph.

The 'Holy Angel's' place seems a lovely place. The people there seem to be very nice. Did you go there much or were you living there for a while when you were very sick?

Another thing I found on the internet was that they almost have a cure for HHT, at present they can manage the symptoms, so it's looking good for the future, but I guess that's too late for you now. Was it really an awful sickness? I hope you didn't suffer too much. I don't like it when people suffer. The only person I ever saw suffering before was my Nana before she died in 2000. I was very sad then. I miss her a lot. Will you give her a little peck on the cheek from me, you couldn't miss her, she's the one with the great big smile. Thanks.

What is Heaven really like anyway Grace, is it really as good as people say it is? Is there lots of fruit and nice food there? Do you have to go to school? Do you play football up there? I just love football, Irish dancing, playing the piano and the violin and listening to music. I get the feeling you like these things too, especially listening to music, which is what you did a lot of in the 'Holy Angels' place. Are you a little angel now?

Did you know that the Special Olympics were held in Ireland this year? This is the first year they were held outside America. Ireland was delighted to host it and every town was involved. The opening ceremony was absolutely fantastic. It's a pity you weren't here because you could have taken part in it and maybe we could have met.

Well Grace, I guess I gotta go. Hope the weather is as good up there as it is down here. It's been really good telling you the news. I just wish you could tell me some of your news. Anyway, I will write to you again when I have more news for you. Till then, take care Little Angel.

Love Aphra Ni Chuinneachain,
Scoil Rois,
Carraig Mhachaire Rois,
Co. Monaghan.

P.S. Friends forever

XXX

Dear Grace:

Since you died some good and bad things happened. People have been given life, babies have been born. People have died, people have been murdered and abused. A lot of brilliant and disasterous things have happened to people of all different shapes, sizes and ages. But we have to understand that things happen for a reason, that it is destiny and that we have to try and prevent bad, try to heal the sick and to spread happiness all over the world. So I am going to tell you just a few things that made people laugh and cry, rise and fall, miracles and heartbreaks. I am going to tell you about some new beginnings and dead ends, some happy and sad. So please put aside some time to read about my view of the year, 2003.

A big issue this year was and is the war on Iraq. It was said that Iraq had nuclear weapons. America gave Iraq a time limit to get rid of them and when all the weapons weren't confiscated, America declared war on Iraq. A lot of innocent and guilty people were killed, from news reporters to Iraqis, Americans to British. Hurt was everywhere in Iraq. People got physically and mentally hurt. Children were left without parents, peoples loved ones were killed and billions of tears were shed. The Americans think that Saddam was killed and many rejoiced while some wanted revenge. To this very day peace is being restored in Iraq, houses are being rebuilt. Lives are also being rebuilt, no one has to fear the man who caused them so much hurt or loss. But there needs to and will be a lot of improvements in Iraq and its people.

But not all bad things happened since you died, for example, the first Special Olympics held out of America. It was held right here in Ireland. It was really special and if you had seen it, you would have been as happy as I was for the participants. They had really good sporting talents, were delighted to be representing their Country and they made friends for life. It was a really good experience for them and they'll never forget it. It was an honour to have it held here in Ireland. Every town had its own Country to be host to. The town that I live in, Clonakilty, was host town to Denmark. I had great fun welcoming them to Clonakilty. At school and at home I learnt about the Special Olympics. I watched extracts from the games. Many people from Ireland won medals. Many people not just competitors laughed, cried, sang and danced.

Ireland will never forget the time in 2003 when the Special Olympics were held out of America for the first time. They will remember the time when the

Special Olympics were held in Ireland.

Lately the All-Ireland Hurling final between Cork and Kilkenny was on. Although I do not know the final score, I know that Kilkenny won by just three points. I obviously wanted Cork to win because that is where I always lived and where I still do. A lot of people were disappointed but a lot more were over the moon. The start of the match was a bit disappointing for Cork but we all knew that they tried to do their best. In the end DJ Carey gave a speech on behalf of the team. Many people were cross with him because he based the speech and match around himself.

This year a book was released. A book that was released all over the world to millions of people young and old. The book was written by a lady named J.K. Rowling and the name of this book is Harry Potter and the Order of the Phoenix. This book was so big that a group of boys were caught for stealing pages of the book before it was published. I thought that the book was excellent but the start was a bit boring. I read all the Harry Potter books, some of them four times. I think that J.K. Rowling is a brilliant writer and I will be sad when the Harry Potter series is finished. I am sure that many people are with me when I say that.

This year a priest in Clonakilty parish by the name of Father Gavin, shaved his beard for charity. Father Gavin looks a bit different to me, but I know that he is the same person inside and I know that just because his beard is gone doesn't mean that his love for God is gone. Also this year a priest in Clonakilty parish retired. I was surprised, I don't really know why. Was it because I didn't think a priest like him would retire? Instead of that priest, a new priest arrived to the Parish.

But people didn't just do charitable work in Clonakilty. They do it all over the world. For example, in England there are three programmes that raise money for charity by holding a competition where people ring in to vote and by ringing in they give money to a charity picked by the presenters. I think that these programmes are very enjoyable. Some of the programmes include Celebrity Farm, I'm a Celebrity Get me out of Here, Fame Academy, Red Nose and the Games. I am going to tell you about Fame Academy. This is a programme where celebrities go into an Academy and learn to sing like professionals. They sing to keep their place in the Academy. They are voted out by the viewers ringing in to vote for their favourite celebrity. It goes on over a few weeks and you have to wait to see who wins and who does not. I think that the celebrities are good to go on television and sing even if they can't and maybe, just maybe they might find a hidden talent that they can express themselves in. Maybe they might get a new career or maybe they might get voted out on the first night because they were so bad.

This year I am in sixth class. It is my final year in Primary school. It will be a big change to go into secondary school. I am looking forward to meeting old friends and making new friends. I have a very good and very old friend that is in sixth class now but she is in a different school. Although I have really good friends in this school I also know that I have very good friends in others. I am happy to know all the friends I have made over the years. I know that friends are very important to give you confidence and hope and that you have to do the same for them.

Schools also evolve very often. It is amazing to think back to when our parents were in school. So much has changed since then. O.K., the colour and teachers have probably changed, so have the books, the playground and even the accessories. So much has changed and will change in the near future. Students have also changed, every year old students leave and new students arrive. Many people from one family come, just imagine, your grandmother might have gone to the same school as you did. It would just make you wonder about what is going to happen in the future. Is everything going to change or are our methods going to be kept?

I love sports. For example, swimming, camogie, badminton and I also like tennis. I am in a swimming club and I love it if you ignore the early mornings. I am also in a badminton and camogie club. It is something to do and I like it. I have eleven cats and one dog so as you can guess I am a fan of animals. I love cats, even if it's a tiger or a lion. I live on a farm and I love that as well. So much open space and air and I am just a few minutes from the town. I love my family and where I live. If anything happened to my family I would cry for days and nights forever more.

Every year something new is invented or someone great is born. Things are changed and people become more mature and grow up a bit. People learn a bit more, people make new friendships and strengthen old friendships. We have to try and evolve and grow with the things around us. We have to make changes to stay alive. We have to believe in each other and have faith and hope for the coming years. New things happen for a reason, as I said before its destiny. We need our families and friends just like we need our heart to live, because our family and friends have a very special place in our heart. So here Grace, I am going to leave you but I am sure we will meet again.

Your friend
Norma O'Mahony,
St. Joseph's G.N.S.,
Clonkakilty,
Co. Cork.

Dear Grace:

I hope you are well since the last time I wrote to you. I have been up to so much fun since the last time I contacted you, I'm sure you had a great time too. Now I will start from September 2002 and tell you of all the stories through out the year, month by month and also what happened in my own personal life.

September 2002: *"Kingdom crumble at Croker"*

The pitch of Croke Park was a sea of Orchard as Armagh won their first All-Ireland title against Kerry. The Kingdom of Kerry had a convincing lead at half time but lost it all in the second half as Armagh won 1-12 to 0-14. The celebrations are still going on as I write!

In Hurling, Kilkenny won the Liam McCarthy Cup.
Daniel O'Donnell the most eligible bachelor in Ireland was no more as he announced his wedding date.

It was also announced that October 19 would be the date that the public would go to the polling booths for the second time on the Nice Treaty. This would be the first election on a Saturday, so no day off for the kids. Some constituencies would use electronic voting.

Kids would bring a tear to your eyes as they went back to school. I started 5th class with a new teacher, Mr. Newman. He was an author and we got off on the right foot.

Ireland's soccer team lost in a thriller to Russia, the score was 4-2.

Roy Keane's autobiography hit the bookshelves and I bought the great book.

It was the first anniversary of the 9/11 attacks. Lives were remembered in an emotional service.

October 2002: *"The Beginning"*

I sharpened my pencil and began the letter that would get me an appearance on the Late Late Toy Show. I sent the letter off and hoped for the best, would I get a reply? Days passed by and there was no reply. There was not going to be a reply was my opinion, would I ever fulfil a life ambition to get on T.V.? Then a phone call changed it all. My Mum, Dad and I were sitting down watching Fair City when the phone rang. My Mum talked on the phone and was told by Bill Malone the Late Late researcher that I would have an audition on November 2nd, and I had to bring my favourite toy.

It was make or break for me. For five years I had been involved in the Saint Anne's school pantomime. I had seen it all, you could say I was a panto veteran. Now there was going to be a new director. I went through the audition and 2 weeks later I began rehearsals for my sixth panto. I would be Scratchy (a dwarf) in Snow White and the Seven Dwarfs.

The Irish soccer team fell to another defeat, this time against Switzerland. Soon after, Mick McCarthy stood down as Irish manager. Irish football was in ruins.

The government were having troublesome times as the economy slowed down. The Celtic Tiger had lost his roar and put down his tail.

Ireland voted a resounding Yes! to the Nice Treaty.

Schools around the country started protesting again for better facilities. My school was one of them. October was a busy month.

November 2002 *"The Late Late Story"*

November 2nd arrived and I picked up the bag that carried my two favourite toys, my wrestlers and my Gamecube. My usual taxi man Dermot brought my mum and me to RTE studios in Donnybrook. I stood out of the taxi and I sucked in the RTE air, this was the air I wanted to be in on the 29th November, the day the Late Late Toy show was on. I waited and waited and waited until I finally got called in for the audition. It went well, I just went in for a chat, did I make a good impression? 2 weeks passed with no reply, then the phone rang again…."Hi this is Bill Malone, your son made an almighty impression, and he will be on the Late Late Toy Show. We'll send out some toys and he will demonstrate them." I told my teacher Mr. Newman and my classmates, they were happy for me. November 29th rolled around and I was ready. I brought the box of toys they gave me with me and went with Dermot again. I saw my

friend Ronan on the way, I waved, and he waved. He would see me later on T.V. I arrived at RTE and went straight into rehearsals. It didn't go so well. One of my toys wouldn't work and another was cut. It was all going wrong. But I picked myself up, got a bite to eat, and I was ready. 9.30 p.m. rolled around and I was about to go on, I sucked in the sights, this was a once in a lifetime experience. I went on, Pat Kenny came to me. Everyone in Shankill was watching me. I did well, except they cut my commentary out. I was supposed to do a football commentary about Kerry and Dublin, I was gutted. I went home disappointed, but I will forever remember the 29th of November, even when I'm on my deathbed, I will look back on this experience.

Roy Keane comes to Eason's in Dublin and Cork. I was there to see him in Dublin and I was very lucky to get my book signed.

The weather is average and stocks are good.

December 2002: *"A Hair Shirt Budget"*

Charlie McCreevy stepped out of Dail Eireann; briefcase in hand and finally delivered the annual budget. This budget was a hair shirt budget as expected. The economy is in a bad state and this budget confirmed it.

Football teams resumed training including Kerry. Meanwhile former Kerry football legend Mick O'Dwyer takes charge of Laois. Things start to look up for the midland team.

It is the first Christmas with the euro and looks like people have got used to it, but a lot of people have the same verdict, "The money is hopeless, it's toy money".

In Tae Kwon Do I receive my blue belt after vigorous testing.

I do some shopping in the capital and come back with some bargain buys.

In Dublin's fair city, money is being wasted on a big spike; it is part of the redevelopment of O'Connell Street.

There is trouble in Cork as their hurling and football teams go on strike. They were looking for better facilities. The issue is eventually resolved.

I have a good Christmas getting a lot of presents. 2002 had been kind to me, what was in store for 2003?

January 2003: *"Animals"*

Kerry football manager Paidi O'Shea was not in the good books of the people in his native Kerry. It stated in the Irish Independent that he called his supporters animals, always expecting to win. Maybe he had a few jars on him when he said it! Anyway Paidi denied that he made these comments. The media had a field day with one reporter following him out to Cape Town! Eventually it blew over.

I completed my sixth panto, having a great time. I put in a stellar performance.

The weather is mild and the spike is slowly gathering pace.

Crime figures show some good news and the government introduced a new penalty points system.

A new Credit Union is being built in Shankill and 4 new shops are being built as well.

The national broadcaster RTE announced an increase in the television licence. The increase brought the licence to €150.

School is good and I'm living life to the full.

January was an interesting start to 2003 a year to bring much promise.

February 2003: *"Flying boot"*

Soccer star David Beckham walked around with nine stitches above his left eye. Why? His manager Sir Alex Ferguson was livid after a defeat. In the dressing room afterwards he stood back and kicked the boot that lay in front of him. It hit David. There was a massive commotion; after all it was just a storm in a teacup.

Brian Kerr was appointed Irish soccer manager and he got off to a good start.

The weather is mild and flowers start to blossom. Farmers are busy on the farm.

Dubliners are busy looking for the fugitive, a creation of radio channel 98FM.

Shankill is looking good. Preparations for St. Patrick's Day are happening around the country.

March 2003: *"Irish eyes are smiling"*

Irish eyes were smiling in March as we were given a taste of sunshine.

Many people turned out in the sunshine for the St. Patrick's Day parade in Dublin city. The parade itself was a lavish affair with pop star Samantha Mumba leading the parade. But Dublin wasn't the only place holding parades, with parades being held all around Ireland and America.

It was discovered that T.V. and radio host Pat Kenny earned more than half a million euro. That's even more than our Taoiseach Bertie Ahern. This angered many people.

Crime goes up with more young people being involved in crime and a lot of burglaries. Drink driving is down thanks to the penalty points system.

There are a lot of redundancies in the lovely country of Ireland. There are more people queuing up for the dole. It is desperate.

Mickey Joe Harte is chosen to represent Ireland in the 2003 Eurovision Song Contest in Latvia. Would he follow Dana, Johnny Logan and Linda Martin and bring the Eurovision crown back to where it belongs in Ireland?

March was a good month; they year 2003 was going good so far….

April: *"Hands down"*

Since 1999 I had won gold medals in a poetry feis, but this year it changed. I went on and said my poem. I made a gesture with my hands, which proved clinical. The adjudicator announced the results: I finish a close second with marks being deducted for using my hands. I was gutted. I picked myself up and went shopping to buy myself some Gamecube games.

I had a student teacher called Mr McCarthy; I play an April fools joke on him. He left but we didn't know our paths would cross later on in the year.

Soaps are good with enthralling storylines, especially in Coronation Street.

Man. United look to have the advantage in the Premier League Title race, while in the European cup they treat the public to a classic match with Real Madrid.

Jaunting cars start to come back in Killarney after the winter break. The Americans always love a ride!

Riga in Latvia prepares for the Eurovision song contest. Singers such as Joe Dolan, Daniel O'Donnell and Johnny McEvoy are busy singing all around Ireland and Europe while comedians Brendan Grace and Brendan O'Carroll are busy preparing new jokes for the upcoming tourist season.

A sunny Easter passes by - now it's time for summer or was it?

May 2003: *"Mayday blues"*

May was supposed to be the first month of summer, but it was more like the first month of winter. The rain poured down for most of May. Many people rushed to the travel agents to book a holiday in the sun thinking it would be a bad summer but they would be proved wrong.

Mickey Harte sang in the Eurovision song contest with his song "We've got the world". He did Ireland proud and finished a respectable 11th. Turkey won the contest after stiff competition from Belgium and Russia. Britain received no points in the contest.

I went to my cousin John's 21st birthday party. Young and old gathered for the bash, which went on to the wee hours of the morning. It was a great party.

The Football Championship started again and so did the Hurling Championship. There were some shocks in the early going.

Man United win another Premier League Title.

Favourite children authors John Newman (my teacher) and Jim Halligan launched their new book Seeing Red. It shifts a good few copies on the first day of sales.

More students from France, Italy and China come to Ireland to learn English. This boosts tourism in Ireland.

June 2003: *"A June to remember"*

The last week in June was a week to remember as for the first time the Special Olympics were held outside of America, they were held in Erin's Green Isle itself, Ireland! The Special Olympics are for mentally disabled people, for one week they participate in different sports. They are put in different categories depending on their ability. The week started off with the opening ceremony with many celebrities turning out for the event. The torch was lit and the games began. I went to one of the events myself, to see the badminton with my classmates. I also went to the closing ceremony, which was a great event. The Special Olympics was a great event and wouldn't be complete without the volunteers.

On June 21st the fifth Harry Potter book was released. Many people queued up all night to get the book.

Man. United were prepared to sell David Beckham to Real Madrid.

Kerry start their football campaign with a ruthless annihilation of Tipperary while Laois beat Dublin. Spirits were high in the O'Moore County. After being on strike in December, Cork hurlers come back and win the Munster crown.

You would stand back and smile as kids ran out of school without a care in the world and I was one of them. It was now time to relax.

This was a June to remember!

July 2003: *"Summer time at last"*

It was about time Ireland got some sunshine! The sun blazed down on many days in July.

Special Olympic athletes returned home after their accomplishments.

The local pub holds its annual festival in which the kids enjoyed themselves in the daytime and the adults enjoyed a good drink with great entertainment at night time.

The Taoiseach Bertie Ahern breaks up with his long-term partner Celia Larkin. She quickly forgets about the split and starts to date a cobbler. Meanwhile Bertie's daughter Georgina is preparing for her wedding to childhood sweetheart Westlife's Nicky Byrne.

David Beckham moved to Real Madrid for 25 million thus ending his love affair with Manchester United.
Kerry won another Munster title with the destruction of Limerick while Laois won their first Leinster title in 57 years. There were frantic scenes afterwards on the way back to Laois.
I was looking forward to my holidays in Lanzarote and I was starting to pack my bags.

The people who weren't going off to the sun were enjoying a rare Indian summer in Ireland.

August 2003: *"Roses, Cockroach's and Sunshine"*

August was a busy month and it started off with two double headers at Croke

Park. The first day, Tyrone and Armagh enjoyed victories while the second day Kerry won in emphatic style and Donegal and Galway finished all square. Donegal won the replay.

I go to see the film Veronica Guerin. It is a brilliant film, a very exciting and moving tale with brilliant acting. All the actors were Irish except one.

The day arrived for me to go on holidays. I awoke at 4am ready to go. When my family and I arrived at the Dublin Airport we were told there would be an eight-hour delay. We were supposed to go out at 8am now we would go at 3pm. So we waited and waited and waited. Then we found out the flight would not go until 7pm. This was bordering on the ridiculous. I told the travel agent (who will remain nameless) that this was not good enough. They didn't care what I had to say. Then the killer blow came, 23:00hrs would be the time of the flight, but this was not possible. Arrecife (Lanzarote) airport closes at midnight. We go to the travel agents, there's a crowd there. After several lies we are finally told we would not be flying out till the next day. What about the people from Cork, Galway and Cavan? They had to go home and so did I. We came back the next day, there was more lies, tears, shouting and delays. Eventually Airport police had to be called in. We finally flew out at 3.30pm. That's 31 hours after we were originally to fly out. We finally got to Lanzarote and had a great time. I went to the pool and beach. There were loads of Irish bars but I ended up going to a British bar where I amazed everyone with my Karaoke skills. It was great craic! I went on a camel, I was up on volcanoes, I was on a cruise, I had a great time in Lanzarote. One night we went back to the apartment and there were some unexpected visitors in the room, Cockroaches! My mum went straight down to reception and we moved rooms. I left Lanzarote with loads of good memories and bad!

The day after I returned from Lanzarote I went to Croke Park to see Kerry play Tyrone. It was a rubbish match and dirty match in which Tyrone won. Pat Spillane described it best by saying it was "puke football". A post-mortem was called in Kerry as the county was in mourning.

Then I went to Killarney in Co. Kerry. My family and I stayed in a lovely B & B called the Harp. Up the road in the Gleneagle hotel there was top class entertainment with Brendan Shine, Keith and the Showband show, Brendan Grace and more. I met footballing legend Tom Spillane (Pat's brother). I met all the Roses from the Rose of Tralee including the winner Orla Tobin The Dublin Rose. A lot of them were going home after a great week in the Kingdom. The festival continued. I also went on a jaunting cart.

Now it was time to go home and go to school.

In other news: Georgina Ahern and Nicky Byrne finally tied the knot. Security was tight for the event. Cork and Kilkenny would contest the hurling final while Armagh and Tyrone would contest the football final, an all Ulster affair.

August was a busy month, a month never to be forgotten.

September 2003: *"Cork fail to skin the cats"*

The rebels of Cork failed to skin the Kilkenny cats. With a great minor match to set the scene everything was ready for hurling's big day. After an atrocious first half, the second half was a classic but in the end Kilkenny won. The great D.J. Carey lifted the Liam McCarthy Cup after a troublesome week personally.

RTE created a new reality T.V. show called Celebrity Farm. Eight Celebrity Farmers went on the farm and they were Twink (actress), Paddy O'Gorman (reporter), Mary Coughlan (singer), Kevin Sharkey (artist), Mary Kingston (kids T.V. presenter), Tamara Gravasoni (2002 Rose of Tralee), Gavin Lambe Murphy (model), George McMahon (Mondo from Fair City, actor). George won. The show was a bundle of laughs with love sparks between George and Tamara. T.V. ratings show over half a million people watched the show nightly.

The Late Late Show was entering a new term hosted by Pat Kenny but now it had competition, the Dunphy Show, hosted by outrageous ex-footballer Eamon Dunphy. The two engaged in a slagging match and there was a lot of media hype. The night came and both shows done well. I watched The Dunphy Show. When it came down to the ratings Kenny trounced Dunphy. Hopefully Dunphy will fight back.

Swedish politician Anna Lind was killed just days before the Swedish referendum on the euro.

Hurricane Isabelle hit parts of America.

Tickets went on sale for the Daniel O'Donnell concert in the Point. They are quickly sold out.

Kids grim faces conveyed their feelings as they went back to school.

I started sixth class with my former student teach Mr McCarthy. We have slagging matches as he is from Limerick and I follow Kerry. Hopefully he will be able to keep my classmates and I under control!

Shankill is looking good with two new shops and a barbershop.

September was a good month for Pat Kenny and the cats, but not for kids and Eamon Dunphy!

Well Grace, I tried to the best of my ability to bring you up to date of what happened in the last year. If I left anything out please don't be too hard on me.

I had some great times over the past twelve months and I have loved sharing them with you. This past twelve months have been crazy and now you know.

Best Wishes

Yours Truly,

Your friend always,
Barry Lenihan,
St. Anne's N.S.,
Shankhill,
Dublin.

Dear Grace:

We all miss you very much, but in a way you are not really gone because no matter what happens you will always be in our hearts. How is Heaven? Are the clouds made of ice cream? Does God have a big long beard? And do you have to go to mass when you're in Heaven, because to be brutally honest, I sometimes find mass a little boring! I had better stop asking you questions but could you do me a favour? Could you please tell my two Grandads I said hello, oh and tell my Godmother I miss her very much. I'll describe my Grandads and Godmother to you so that you know what they look like. My Grandads are a bit old so you might find them sitting in big armchairs watching stuff like the Sunday Game Live and the Ford Football Special. My godmother is a beautiful angel wearing a long, white and silky dress you might find her sitting on a cloud playing a harp. Now I'll tell you what's been going on down here on Earth. In Dublin they've built this huge spike I think it's either called, "The Millennium Spire" or "The Spike". I think it is the most crappiest thing that has ever been built in Dublin. What's the point of having a great big spiky thing in the middle of Dublin, if you ask me I think they should put some sort of platform at the top of it and let people go bungee jumping off it! That would make anyone's trip to Dublin memorable. We also had the All Ireland hurling final in September. It was Cork playing Kilkenny and after a tense and exciting match, Kilkenny were declared the champions. I hate to tell you bad news Grace but I should tell you that earlier on in the year 2003, despite the protests of people all over the world, America declared war on Iraq. I just didn't understand why were the people of Iraq being punished for the things that their leader had done? And even after the war had ended a while later, they hadn't even captured Iraq's leader Saddam.

Did you know that a magician called David Blaine is staying in a small narrow glass box, living only on water for forty-four days and nights? I'm not sure what he's accomplishing by doing this. I've heard that some nasty people threw eggs at his box and that someone even tried to cut off his water supply. I'm not sure if you know this Grace but because of you having HHT, lots more people are surviving from it! And for that you must be very, very, very, very proud.

J.K Rowling released her new Harry Potter book. It's called, "The Order of the Phoenix". I've read it and I think that it is absolutely fantastic! I'm sure you heard about the tragic events that took place on the eleventh of September 2001.

We mourned for those whose loved ones lost their lives on the anniversary. Unfortunately another bad thing happened this year. Doctors discovered an outbreak of a new disease called SARS. They discovered the outbreaks in China, Japan, and Canada. It was a contagious disease that unfortunately killed many innocent people, thankfully it's now been put under control.

In my family my Granny turned a whopping 93! In our park a massive purple beech tree toppled over in a storm. It was one of the biggest purple beech trees in the whole of Ireland! Luckily, the people who run the park had planted two other purple beech trees earlier in the year as they could see that the bigger tree would die anyway. In Riga, Latvia, the Eurovision song contest 2003 was held. Although we didn't win it, Ireland's representative Mickey Joe Harte did Ireland proud. I don't mean to ask you more questions Grace, but what's it like being an angel? Does your halo ever fall off? Do you have wings? I sure hope you do because I'd love to be able to fly anywhere I'd like. I'd fly all over Europe, Asia, America, Australia and Africa. I'm in sixth class now and to be honest it feels sort of strange knowing that next September I'll be starting a whole new school! The government are bringing out this new law that will not allow anyone to smoke in any public place. It's coming out next year (2004) and I think it is a very reasonable law because when people smoke they are harming other people around them. Another new law is that if you drop a cigarette butt on the ground you can get fined up to one hundred euro, so they have made this new little portable ashtray that you can clip onto your belt so that you won't be dropping your cigarette butts on the ground. I don't think the little ash trays will really catch on because some people just won't bother with them, because some people are big lazy lumps that eat too much junk from McDonalds but hey, that's just one girl's opinion. Some new songs have been released since you were down here. Here are my favourites, "Where is the Love?" by the Black Eyed Peas. "Bring me to Life" and "Going Under" by Evanescene and "You're so Yesterday" by Hilary Duff. Do you read any books Grace? I'm sure you do. I read lots of books. I like Jacqueline Wilson's books, thrillers and horror books the best, but I'm also very fond of the Nancy Drew books, "the Diary of Anne Frank" and a book called "The Daisy Chain War". I hope that there are libraries up in Heaven because I don't know what I would do if I didn't read books. In school we are learning about all the different religions such as Hinduism, Judaism, Muslims and Buddhism. Hindus have not got one central figure like the way Christians have Jesus Christ, oh no Hindus have heaps of Gods. So in Heaven would there be lots of different sections like different sections for different religions or would all religions be put together and automatically live in peace?

I went on my holidays to Southern France this year to a massive complex. The weather was fantastic and my sister introduced me to a really nice girl called Grace who we both made friends with. In August I went to Dunmore East to the adventure centre and it was really brilliant. We did all sorts of stuff like kayaking rock climbing, pedal boating, orienteering, archery, surf skis and lots of other things.

My hobbies are swimming, reading, acting, tennis, playing the piano, singing and baking. On Saturdays I go to Jesters Stage Academy, play tennis and then I go to choir in the Kilkenny School of Music. It's all really good fun and I do it all with my best friend Sinead. Jesters is really good fun. At it, we do singing, dancing and acting and at the end of the year the whole academy puts on a big show in our local theatre for three days in June. In tennis you play games and matches, which are really good. In choir we sing really cool songs (and don't worry you don't have to wear any long dresses) and do lots of concerts throughout the year.

Another place that I went on holidays was Norway. We stayed in Oslo (the capital of Norway) for a few days then we took a six and a half hour train journey to Bergen. I was really nervous about the train journey because trains are very bumpy and I was afraid I would get sick and spoil my holiday but the train was not a bit bumpy because we were in a first class carriage! It was lovely. It had big comfy chairs and lots of room. The scenery was fantastic, we passed big smooth lakes called fiords and beautiful snow capped mountain. I didn't want to leave the train when we arrived in Bergen! Another great place that I went on holidays to was Tenerife. I think it's been my favourite holiday so far because we went to this brilliant water park called Aqua Park. The Aqua Park had lots of slides and they also did dolphin shows. My brothers, sister, Mum and Dad and I went to see one. I was amazed at what the dolphins could do. So I went to see the second show (they do two shows a day) and sat right up front. The show began and then I noticed that the trainers were picking children from the audience to do tricks with the dolphins. The trainer pointed at me and before I knew it I was boogie boarding in the water with a dolphin. I left the show early to tell my parents what I had just done. On our way out from the park I noticed posters advertising a programme where you could swim with dolphins in the park for a whole day! I picked up a brochure and showed it to my Mum and before I know it the next day I was taking part in the programme "Interaction with Dolphins". That was my best holiday ever.

When I'm older I'd either like to be a marine biologist, a child psychiatrist, a teacher or an actress. What do you want to be when you're older Grace? I bet it's something really nice.

Well I think that I've covered most of the things that've happened and are happening, I hope that you are having a really nice time in heaven flying around the clouds and playing your lovely harp. We will always be thinking of you down here on earth! (No matter what happens!)

Keep on Smiling!

Your great friend

Katie-Pia Moran
St. John of God N.S.,
Kilkenny.

Dear Grace:

How are you in Heaven? I want to know do animals go to heaven or is it just people?

An orang-utan has been born in San Diego zoo. Its mother would not take care of Ciara (the orang-utan) so the zookeepers adopted it. They treated it like a baby. Later that year Ciara was returned to the zoo and another orang-utan named Josephine started to take care of her. But now there was another problem. Ciara had a coin shaped hole in her heart. The zookeepers brought her to the hospital where she became the first animal to undergo open-heart surgery. It was successful even though it will take a while for her to recover but when she does she will be put back in the zoo again.

This year I went to France on holidays in my caravan. We went there on the car ferry. We had to spend the night on the ship. It was brilliant but the cabins were tiny. When we got to France we took a week to travel down to the Pyrenees on the French-Spanish border. We spent a week and a half there. We had a brilliant time. We went to the Huatacam and halfway up the Tourmalet. We went across a mountain in a cable car and a chair lift. Then we walked to the lake and that was Pont Espagne. We spent the rest of our holidays (half a week) going back up to Cherbourg which was a brilliant holiday and I went swimming everyday.

Speaking of swimming, two weeks ago I went to Lilliput in the caravan. Lilliput is a brilliant outdoor adventure centre on Lough Ennell. We went to stay with the I.C.C. (Irish Camping and Caravanning Club). I have a wetsuit and I went swimming everyday even though it wasn't very warm. That was brilliant. Mum brought her canoe and we all had a turn. David's friend Blane came for a visit. David (my brother in case you haven't guessed) and Blane went blackberry picking and they got lots and lots. Blane stayed the night in the tent with David and Joe (my other brother) and I slept in the caravan. On Tuesday we made blackberry tart. It was delicious and we ate it all on Tuesday. Are there hills and lakes and mountains and rivers in heaven?

This weekend we went off in the caravan again but this time we went to Drumgoff in the Wicklow Mountains. It was amazing even though it rained all weekend. On Saturday we went to the Dad of the Year competition in Dublin. We didn't win but it was still great fun. We got a Weetabix hamper full of cereal. When we got back Mum and I and two of Mum's friends went for a

animals in heaven

walk. We walked to a place where they are making a film called King Arthur. We had something to eat when we got back. On Sunday we walked up to this really high rock called Michael Dwyer's Rock. From there we could see the caravan site which is in the army barracks. Michael Dwyer was in the I.R.A. and the rock was his lookout. Whenever he saw the barracks empty he would tell the I.R.A. and they would race in and burn it down and then hide in the mountains when the army got back. Were you interested in history? I am, but I hate it in school because there are too many dates and names to remember.

The Dad of the Year competition is another competition I've entered. I nominated my dad and he was one of the fifteen finalists picked. We went to Croke Park in Dublin where we and had a buffet lunch and dessert. For lunch I had chips and chicken nuggets and for dessert there was chocolate profiteroles, which are delicious. Then they called up all the dads and they had to make a speech. Each dad got a hamper and a certificate. The kids got a tomb raider can, a box of K-nex and a toy chicken. The children could also get their face painted and there was a balloon modeller as well. I got flowers painted on my face and David was a lion. Did you ever win any competitions when you were down here?

Penalty points have been introduced in Ireland this year. They are given if you are caught speeding or if anyone in the car isn't wearing a seatbelt. If you get more than twelve points you will not be allowed to drive for three years. It's a good idea because it makes drivers slow down which means less crashes, which is good news. But it's not absolutely brilliant news for me because now mum can only carry four people if I go in the front, so hopefully no one will need a lift to my birthday party or anywhere else either. It's also bad for football matches because now even more parents have to bring us there because everyone needs a seatbelt now. Do you know anyone in heaven who died in a car crash?

My birthday this year was brilliant. I was twelve this year and I invited all my friends. It was Joe's birthday soon too and his party was the same day as mine.

I didn't mind because Anna and Maeve were there (Anna is our cousin and Maeve is her best friend) and Maeve is really cute. We had a pizza (yuk) and sausage rolls (yum) and lots of crisps. There was of course birthday cake that I had made and iced myself. It was great fun. My best friend Leanne was at the party. Who was your best friend and do you have another one in heaven?

I hate going to the dentist and so do all my friends. It's even worse for me because I have an orthodontist and I have to get braces. I have already had two different types of braces, which nobody had ever seen before. I have also had to have two teeth taken out and that hurt a lot. Soon I have to get train-track braces but oh well at least my teeth will be straight. Do people in heaven have bad teeth too or does everyone have perfect teeth? Did you have to get teeth out when you were alive?

I'm in such a rush to finish this. The deadline to be sent in is Tuesday the 30th. I hate deadlines, like in school when Miss says we only have till eleven o'clock to finish our work, like on forms that mum fills out for us that have to be back in school tomorrow or deadlines on competitions like this one and you don't have time to finish or nobody posts your entry in time. Or like at our Christmas concert when we only had a few days to learn all our lines. I wish that there were no deadlines, that everybody could do things at their own pace, but then no competitions could ever end and no work would get done so maybe it is a good thing that there are deadlines. But that doesn't change the fact that I hate them, hate them, hate them.

Our school tour this year was mega. Robert, Ciaran and Aidan sang the whole way to Dublin on the bus. First was Kilmainham Jail. That was really cool. There we saw the place James Connolly was shot with all the other 1916 Rising leaders. We were allowed to go into some cells but most were still locked. We saw the children's exercise yard where the children had to walk around in a circle

without making noise for hours. Next came the zoo. We all jumped in fright when the leopard pressed himself right against the glass in front of us. I loved watching the baby orang-utans and the baby seals were really cute (they sure can swim fast). When we were going home the bus was late. By the time the bus appeared it had rained for half an hour and even worse my liquorice strings were all gone long ago. Humours were really bad until AT LAST we stopped at a shop. Like an army of savages we entered the shop. We scared the poor shopkeeper to death (only joking). We all got the kind of trash no mother would ever allow (Stinger bars, black jacks etc, etc.). It was the best school tour ever.

And now the end. I'm sure you're worn out reading this rambling letter but I was mad to tell you all the latest news. I'd love to know what the craic is like up there with you. I really hope you are happy and not too bored with the angels and fluffy white clouds, or is it candyfloss? It's probably not at all like that maybe you'll appear to me in a vision - no! Scrap that thought, way too scary.

Yours Sincerely

Martina Boyd, 6th Class
St. Finnians,
Co. Meath

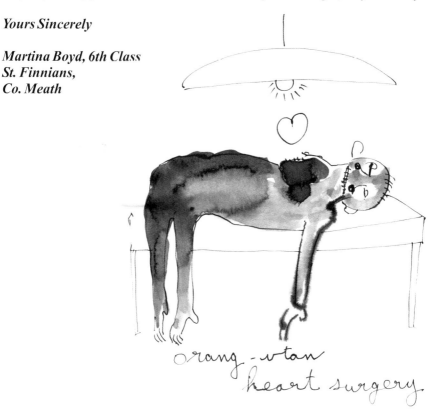

orang-utan
heart surgery

78

Dear Grace:

How are you? I often wonder what it is like up there in heaven looking down on everyone. Maybe some day you could write back to me and tell me what it is like up in heaven. There has been a lot happening here on earth. In 2001 a mad man called Osama Bin Laden ordered his men to crash into the Twin Towers in New York. As the planes crashed into the towers it set fire to them and the whole thing collapsed. Thousands and thousands of people died. Now every year on the eleventh of September we have one minute's silence to show our respect.

Last year Brazil won the World Cup. Ireland was left number sixteen. The games that Ireland did play were really tough. We had to play without Roy Keane. A couple of days ago I went to my friend's birthday party. It was really fun. There was a magician. Yesterday, I went to my other friend Aoife's house. I have a pony called Champ. My brother has a pony called Lilly and my Mum has a horse called Flame. We also have a dog named Toby and a bird called Tiki.

I have a brother called Jack aged eleven and one sister called Mary Kate aged four. I am ten years old. For the summer I went to Florida, USA, for two weeks. It was great fun; we went to Orlando. There were lots of theme parks and lots of cool rides. On the first day we went to Sea World. We saw lots of animals. There were dolphins, sharks, birds, seals, penguins, polar bears, whales and lots more. We went to Disney's Epcot on another day and that was really good. One day we went to a water park called Blizzard Beach. It had the highest, fastest water slide in the world. We went to Magic Kingdom and that was my favourite one of all. It had cool rides. I went on Space Mountain, Big Thunder Mountain and Splash Mountain. We went down to Clearwater on Tampa Bay. That was exciting. The beach was nice and sandy and the water was clear and warm. Then we finally came home. I was kind of glad to come home because I missed my dog.

It must be really hard for you Grace to be missing out on all the wonderful things in life. Sometimes it is nice to go on holidays or on day outings but I really just like the simple things in life, like riding my pony or playing with my dog. I love my pony a lot and I love to ride my pony. I like to canter freely around the field. I also like jumping my pony. I like to ride around with my Mum and her horse. Other times I go golfing with my Dad. I like art and drawing. I draw pictures of my pony. I also like to paint pictures. I play hockey in the autumn, winter and spring. I really do love to play hockey. I play with Railway Union Hockey Club.

The All Ireland hurling final was on today. Kilkenny and Cork were playing. It was a really good hurling match and I enjoyed it. It seemed to go on for ages. There was finally a winner. Kilkenny won in the end.

How do you get on in heaven Grace? Do you like it up there looking down on everyone? I have always wondered what it is like in heaven. Is it lonely or is it fun? Are there lots of people or is it just you? Do you wish you were still alive with your family? I could not imagine being separated from my family. Sometimes people argue with their family. If I did not have my family I would not be me. My family are part of who I really am. Can you see your family from heaven? Do you miss them even more when you see them? I bet they miss you as much as you miss them. Do you ever wish you could come back again? What would you do if you could come back? Where would you like to live? What age would you like to be if you did come back? If you came back young would you like to go to school? If you were an adult would you go to work? Have you got a body or are you a spirit? Does everyone speak the same language or do you even speak to each other? Are there any young people to be friends with? What do you do all day? Something I always wanted to know is are there any animals in heaven or do they have their own heaven? If there are animals in heaven please say hello to my cousin's pony Misty who died two years ago. Have you met God? What is he like? Does he live in heaven with you? Do you have to eat in heaven?

I have asked you a lot of questions now and I suppose you want to know what is going on here. My little sister Mary-Kate started school this year. She looks really cute in her new uniform. There is a new series of books out called Harry Potter. There are five books published about him. He is a wizard in them. There are two movies out. There are going to be one movie made for each book.

I am in fifth class and I have a nice teacher this year. She is new to the school. I am learning the tin whistle. The Special Olympics were on in June. The opening night was really nice. There was a concert on in Croke Park. The Corrs were at it and so were U2. There were

Toby   Tiki

people from all over the world there, and there was a special swimming pool opened for it. It was fifty metres long. They had swimming, horse riding, athletics and gymnastics as well as many other sports.

I watched "It Takes Two" yesterday. Do you remember that one? It is quite old. There was a programme on for one week called "Celebrity Farm". It was really good. There were eight celebrities living in a farmhouse for one week and they had to do chores on the farm. You voted for the person you want off the farm. They had to do challenges, one each day. One person went off the farm each day also. The funniest challenge was when they had to be in pairs of two and one person sat in the wheelbarrow and the other person pushed. The person pushing was blindfolded. The person in the wheelbarrow had to give the directions. They had to go up, get a bucket of milk and take it back to the finish line. Last year's Rose of Tralee was in Celebrity Farm. The Rose of Tralee was on this year and the Dublin Rose won. There was a festival and a fun fair. I was in Kerry at the time and I really enjoyed it. That is all my news for now. I enjoyed writing to you. I hope to write to you again soon.

Nancy

XXX

Nancy Kelleher,
Scoil Mhuire,
Sandymount,
Dublin.

Dear Grace:

It is weird for me to write this letter because I've never written to anyone in Heaven before. I am sorry you had to die so young, it must have been terrible. My name is Tom Healy, I'm from Tralee, Co Kerry and I am twelve years old. Here are a few things that happened, both personal and worldwide in 2003. But first I need to ask you a few questions about Heaven; do you have television in heaven?

Do you have the "Sky" channel? How often do you get to meet the boss? Do you play sports in Heaven? Roughly, what is the population? Will you be able to reply to my letter? WILL I HAVE THE RIGHT ADDRESS???

Enough questions.....

2003 was pretty uneventful world wide but a few exciting things happened in my life.

My Mom is always telling me to "watch the news" but the only thing that stood out in my mind was the war in Iraq. President George Bush (I'm not his number one fan) declared war on Iraq and Saddam Hussein in April, and this led to a lot of people being killed, more Iraqis than Americans. Now it is September and people are still being killed.

Much more interesting from my point of view was as a Christmas present my brother and I got A TRIP TO OLD TRAFFORD...Manchester United were to play Chelsea and we had prime location tickets.

After a long, hard battle, in the second minute of injury time in the second half Diego Forlan grabbed the winning goal. With that, Roy Keane ran to Alex Ferguson who was sitting in front of us and waved a victory salute to all.

When we met Mom later and told her all about it she told us that she had written a letter to Roy Keane telling him that we were going to the match that day. She told him our seat numbers, she told him our hair colour, she told him what colour our jackets would be, she even told him our phone number. She hoped if he had time he might acknowledge us somehow, the 'salute' seemed he had remembered.

Anyway our trip to Manchester ended and we came home, depressed that it had ended but delighted with the victory.

Thrown down on the couch the next night watching television only half-heartedly we were disturbed by the phone, me, being the youngest was given the job of answering the interruption and this is what happened;

ME: "hullo"
VOICE: "is that you Evan?"
ME: "no, this is Tom who is speaking please?"
VOICE: "this is Roy Keane"
ME: "ehhh who is speaking please?"
VOICE: "this is Roy Keane"
ME: "pardon?"
VOICE: "THIS IS ROY KEANE"

Then I put my Mom on the phone, all I could hear her say was "now Joe (a family friend) stop messing this minute Joe..Joe, oh my God it is Roy Keane!!! Quick get your Dad tell him Roy Keane is on our phone". Just so happened he had only just opened the letter my Mom had written and was phoning to apologise that he had missed us when we were in Manchester. If ever we were going to go again we were to let him know and he would try his very best to meet us. What a phone call! What was really funny was that the victory salute wasn't aimed at us at all.

It was hard to beat that in other exciting news but in May I spotted a competition and as my pocket money was running short and the prize was €100 (I needed to win badly). I wrote a story on a given theme; "The Queen of the Wasps". It was hard but my Mom helped me and after a lot of used up paper I won the competition. My pocket was full again. I got my photo taken for national and local newspapers. My Grandparents bought me a typewriter as a combined birthday and congratulations gift.

Not long after winning that competition, holiday time arrived.

For the past eight years my family have gone to Turkey for our summer holidays. I love it. I like the people over there, they are very friendly, I love the weather, I love the food. I love the place that we stay in it is called "Pine Club" and we hire a villa with our own pool and a view of the Greek islands all surrounded by pine trees. Sometimes frogs come into our pool. My Mom describes it as a "little piece of heaven". Is she right Grace? Nearly every night we go into Kusadasi town to have a meal, we go on a funny, crowded minibus called a "dolmus". Very near where we stay is a town called Ephesus an ancient town of ruins from thousands of years ago, a bunch of very old rocks and stones…my Dad loves it. It is the town that St Paul wrote all his letters to the citizens who lived there, we hear it as the gospel in mass some Sundays, "A letter from St Paul to the Ephesians". Grace, could you ask him if they ever wrote back??? Ha ha! Also nearby is a village called Selcuk. This is where

John brought our Lady immediately after the crucifixion of Christ. They had to go in a hurry and in secrecy. From this very place she ascended into Heaven. What is really lovely is that the Turkish people, even though they are Muslims have great respect for the Blessed Virgin as the mother of the prophet Jesus. Funny how in some parts of the world different religions can live together. Grace, have you ever been to Kerry? It is not as sunny as Turkey but the people are as friendly. Last August my family and me went to a small fishing village called Dingle in West Kerry. And guess what? The sun shone. Except for one day, that was the day we went to see "Fungi". "Fungi" is a bottle-nosed dolphin who lives in Dingle Bay. He has been living there for twenty years. He loves to get loads of attention from the visitors, who go out to see him on boats.

Another day in Dingle, we went to the Great Blasket island to see the famous Irish writer "Peig Sayers" house: more like a cottage. There is no electricity or phones on the island which means no television!!! I don't know about you Grace but there is no way I'd be able to survive there!

One day we walked on "the edge of the world". It is supposed to be the closest point in Ireland to America. After that we went to Paudi O'Shea's bar and saw the man himself. He was depressed after Kerry's defeat from Tyrone in the all Ireland semi-final. Once we arrived home from Dingle it was nearly time to go back to school! When the day came it was not as bad as I thought it would be. My teacher is sane enough. His name is Mr P Lenihan. It is weird to be in 6th class. Grace I have sort of a wish list for you to give to God (if you can, please):

1. Please could you help United to win the treble this year.
2. Please could you stop the war in Iraq.
3. Please will you make Mr Lenihan not to give us too much homework this year.
4. Please will you bring Sam back to the Kingdom for 2004! Thanks!
5. Could you please say hi to my Grand Dad Michael from Tom.

I know these might be tall orders, but please can you try your best. I never met my grand father but anyone I meet always tells me he was a 'real gentleman' and I am supposed to look like him too.

Oh yes Grace I am so busy talking about all the things that happened to me that I nearly forgot to tell you. I have one brother, his name is Evan and he is older than me, will you ask God to help him in his junior cert this coming June? I also have a dog called Tramp. My Dad says sometimes he thinks Tramp has no brain. I also have a hamster called Roxy. My other hamster died last July, you didn't come upon him did you? His name is Bono and he was great fun.

Well Grace, that's the news from Earth. I hope you get a laugh from it. Please write back if this is possible. If not maybe you could send me some kind of sign to say you got this letter and all is o.k. I hope you are not too lonely up there. Hopefully I won't see you for a long time yet. Give my regards to all in 'Nirvana'

Tom Healy,
Holy Family N.S.,
Tralee, Co. Kerry.

P.S. I'm not quite sure what address to put on the envelope when sending this so I hope when I make a final decision it will reach you.

Dear Grace:

How are you doing? I'm fine. You won't believe what's gone on down here on earth this past year, but let's hear about you first. Did you pass your flying test for your angel's wings yet? I saw a rainbow previously and imagined you passed with flying colours. So how is your mansion in Angel Grove? Is the scenery too cloudy or is it the exhaust fumes from the cloud cars? Have you seen my Uncle up there? He passed away young like you, and I never got to see him. I can't but imagine how the pain sustained when you lose a loved one. So, how did your Junior Cert go? Was maths hard? I mean there is algebra and denominators and yes I will stop boring you with school. So, as I promised, I shall now inform you with what has happened during this previous year.

First in line is the war in Iraq, known as the second Gulf War. Thousands of people in Sydney, London, Dublin and indeed all over the world tried to stop the War. On the billboards, signs and notices reading such phrases as "no to war" and "we've told you Bertie, now you tell Bush" (as in Bertie Ahern and George Bush). Now a friend of mine made a good point previously. He said, "I doubt Bush and Blair would've gone out and risked their lives, they're only the ones who are giving the orders". Sadly they went ahead with the war because they got information from their intelligence that Iraq could deploy weapons of mass destruction, which could cause biological harm within forty-five minutes which the media think is a lie yet nobody will know the truth because I never think MI6 would release such evidence. The British and American forces bombed the capital, Baghdad and the nearby city of Qatar killing hundreds of people and destroying countless buildings and palaces. And all to overthrow a regime run by Saddam Hussein. Let me jog your memory about him. He's evil, cruel and punishing. In fact you cannot fully describe his personality. You'll have to look deeper, for example, his sons Uday and Quasay. Quasay was heir of the throne and he enjoyed human suffering and Uday was ruthless and vicious in all departments. They met their cruel fate when a raid on a palace found their charred remains. Well do you think they should've gone ahead with the war at the price of the casualties of men, women and children alike? I now think Iraq is more vulnerable to an invasion than ever before mainly because of its overwhelming oil supply. It's a real shame because Iraq holds such wonders as the Gardens of Babylon and their museums (now plundered) held the first forms of writing.

Well yet again I must change to another subject. It was previously the anniversary of something special. But not in a good kind of way. It was the

Flight tosting

EVA 6YRS

anniversary of the most depressing and sorrowful date in known history. It was September the eleventh. It was when Osama Bin Laden hired men to crash planes into the Twin Towers, The Pentagon and one plane crashed into a field in Pittsburgh which was heading for the White House in Washington D.C. I can still remember that very day. I was walking down to the local jewellers accompanied by my brother and my mother to get my sister, Clare a present for her Junior Cert (which took place the next day) when we noticed the shopkeeper was pale. My mother asked, "hard day?" The man replied, "heard the news?" He then turned up the radio, "disaster has struck in New York as the Twin Towers have collapsed," said the news correspondent in long sobs. I was awestruck. I'm nearly crying so let's move on. But to what? I'm coming up short with ideas.

Oh I got one. Now I'm moving on to …ME! I can't believe I didn't do this subject first. Well, (since I hate to be anonymous) I'll introduce myself but not yet. Oh, you've forced me to it! My name is Adam Pettigrew. I am ten years old and live in a quaint little semi-detached house in Dublin. (Don't gloat just because you're living in a solid gold mansion). I bet you think it's kind of "uncool" because of my very rare obsession of writing. I have two brothers and one sister. My older brother Daniel is currently working at a part time job at Iceland. Well not the country Iceland, the industry. My sister Claire is nocturnal. She only comes out of her bedroom for materials such as paints and pencils, meals, or the twenty-minute shower each morning! A quick summary of my sister is that she's a kind, funny teenager and she pursues a good reputation for her university. (I'm not sure if it is parties attended or school days!) But all in all she's a seventeen year old and she's my sister and I love her. Next is my younger brother, Jack. He's such a pain!!! I guess I'm just another blank figure in his idea of "play time". But as a seven year old he is sooo easy to manipulate and my wish is indeed his command. But I should talk about his qualities. He's really energetic and is okay at his schoolwork. He is really moany and it is an older brother's duty to annoy him. But I get annoyed by an even bigger pain. The heir to the place of "the man of the house position" Daniel. My older brother (and pain) Daniel I think I've mentioned him already in this letter. He's the one who is always looking out for us or just merely playing with us on the PS2. And my parents? Oh, well I guess it would be indeed impossible to have better parents. By the way, have you seen my dog up there? Sniff, I miss you Joey. He was only a pup when I was born. I think he ran away because I thought he was a horse and used to jump on him and say "giddy up". Huh. Well I got a new dog and his name is Harvey. That really boosts the memory. He got hit by a car whilst chasing some thieves. All for a good cause of course. I still have that bike he saved for me. The thieves dropped it as they made their getaway on foot. Big mistake. I don't think I have mentioned I had a single storey room added to my semi-detached house over the summer. The builders were here for around two months bolting this and plastering that. I was forced to stay at my auntie's house, watching TV for about six hours on end then tearing my sweaty back from the chair to get myself a drink of orange. But it didn't even start yet. The builders left a huge mess and do it yourself mayhem. We all had to pitch in to do the chores my sister designed. My brothers worked buckets of sweat off and I just started screaming at anyone who was either sleeping on the job or lazily slopping paint everywhere. This cleaning frenzy is still in operation to this very day. I received a Windows ninety-five off my Godmother Rita and I am always trying to clear the game Solitaire.

When you get to a certain age, you begin to say to yourself, "what shall I be?" I want to be an astronomer to study the midnight sky and the mysteries it may well hold. But for now I guess I cannot pursue my dream until I complete school. But I can still prepare by obtaining knowledge that others can only wish for. Oh, yes I can picture myself now standing victoriously on a huge platform as the ultimate ruler of the world! Muhahahaha haa! Oops, did I write that down? Well I guess I'm drawing near to the end of this letter so in my defence I say I do not plan to take over the world I plan to leave this letter on a note of appreciation. To whom you ask? Why you of course, no question about that. Now I know you're bombarded and I know this may not stand out much but you've listened to my woes, my refurbishment, my personal facts and my hopes and feelings. Grace, you are loved by family and friends alike and they still love you till this day and even though you tragically passed away that doesn't change a thing. Grace, you're a hero. Thanks to you now kids who once lived in fear can remember your face, now a shining beacon of hope. Now those who suffer from HHT can now live. WE now think of you on cloud nine smiling down on us as we remember you as the "Angel of the Rainbow". You're in our prayers.

WRITE SOON

Adam Pettigrew,
St. Peter's N.S.,
Phibsborough,
Dublin.

P.S. Does St Peter make a fuss at the gates? Hope you're well.

Dear Grace:

Hi! Firstly, I should start by briefly introducing myself because I don't believe that you comprehend who I am. My name is Stefania Stroiescu, but most people call me Stephany since I would rather be called that. I come from a country in the east of Europe, which is called Romania. When I was eight and a half years old, my family (mum, dad and sister) and I moved to Ireland. We lived in Dublin for one year, where I went to St. Matthew's National School. While there, I made a few friends, one of them being my best friend, Roisin Murphy. I moved to Skerries in the year 2001, where I'm currently attending Scoil Realt na Mara, which is very near the sea; therefore, we often see screeching sea gulls flying above our heads.

I have just started sixth class on the first of September this year. I'm very apprehensive about the Entrance Exam coming up in February, which is the same month as my birthday. I have been talking about it so much since we started school that I'm starting to get on my nerves, probably my friends' as well. Oh no, there I go talking about it again! I just can't help myself. But, even though I'm taking the Entrance Exam this year, I have other things that I can look forward to. For example, we're having our confirmation at the end of this year. Well I'm not actually because I'm not Catholic, but luckily, I'm not the only one. Anyhow, it will be fun trying to learn to step dance along with all my classmates. I can just imagine us now!

We're also going to Point Depot near Christmas (7th December) this year to sing different collections of songs along with other schools. We've already heard a few of the songs that we're going to sing. It will probably be fun.

Anyway, how does it feel living so high up in the scenic crystal blue sky, sometimes covered in its milky-white fluffy clouds? Do you get to fly around all day with all the other angels? Do you have many friends? What kinds of things do you do there most of the time? Do you have to go to school or not? How is God? It must be wonderful up there!

I will try to fill you in on most of the things that have happened this year, since I think that you would like to know everything about them. I know that many people wrote to you last year as well but I want to give it an attempt myself this year. Hope you enjoy reading all about them!

Now, where should I start? I'll commence with the Spire or as some people call

it, "The Spike". The Spire is a hollow conical structure and it is located on O'Connell Street, in the place of Nelson's Pillar, which was unfortunately blown up in the year 1966. It rises up to one hundred and twenty metres above O'Connell Street, making it by far the highest building in Dublin city centre. At the base, it is three metres in width, and at the very top, it's only about fifteen centimetres wide. It is made out of stainless steel, which is designed to reflect the changing light of the sky. At night, the surface looks like black satin, while quite early in the morning, it resembles a steely blue colour. In daytime, under bright sunlight and from a distance, it looks like it's unreal and like it's made on a computer. Unfortunately, the building of the Spire cost a lot of money, which I feel, could have been used on other more important things.

Another event that has happened very recently this year, on August 27, was the closest approach of the planet Mars to Earth in the past sixty thousand years, which delighted thousands of stargazers around the whole wide world. Can you imagine that the last time Mars came this close to our planet, the Neanderthals (first humans on Earth) roamed the Earth? Astronomers say that Mars won't be this close to Earth until the year 2287, on August 28, when it will be seventy thousand kilometres nearer. Unluckily, I didn't get to see it, though my friend did through her small telescope. She said that it looked lovely, although she only saw a few red and orange marks on it. Besides, I bet you got the best view of Mars than all of us from the sky!

Something else that happened this year was the release of the book "Harry Potter and the Order of the Phoenix", the fifth one in the series. The book is about Harry's fifth year at Hogwarts's School of Witchcraft and Wizardry, which is packed with exciting adventures and is full of secrets and magic. I don't think you would like me to tell you too much about it since it would spoil the book for you (if you haven't read it yet), so I guess I'll just leave it at that. Though, I can tell you that Joanne Kathleen (J.K.) Rowling succeeds again in creating another fabulous and exciting novel. I read it myself and I thought it was extremely good, even though my favourite one is still "Harry Potter and the Prisoner of Azkaban", the third one in the series. I just wish it didn't end so quickly. Luckily, I can look forward to the sixth book, which is said to be coming out in the year 2005. Anyway, the book is definitely worth reading. Trust me!

The next thing that I'm going to tell you about is regrettably very distressing. It is about the "Columbia" space rocket, the oldest craft in NASA's space shuttle programme, and its tragic accident. It all happened on the date of February 1st this year. As "Columbia" was re-entering the atmosphere, coming back from its sixteen-day mission orbiting the Earth, it started disintegrating into flaming pieces, right above North Texas, killing all seven astronauts on board. It was due to land at the Kennedy Space Centre in Florida fifteen minutes after it fell apart. Many viewers from Earth stated that they first heard a huge bang, after which they described the shuttle as "burning flames in the sky". Television pictures showed several separate vapour trails coming from the crumbled shuttle parts as it flew over Dallas. More than two thousand pieces of debris from the craft fell down to Earth, scattered in many fields. Nobody knows what caused this terrible disaster, but experts suggest that it may probably have been a mechanical or structural problem. Many people were extremely devastated by what happened, especially the families of the shuttle crew. The seven astronauts' names were Rick Husband (USA), William McCool (USA), Kalpana Chawla (USA, but born in India), Laurel Clark (USA), Ilan Ramon (Israel), David Brown (USA) and Michael Anderson (USA). Make sure to greet them from me if you see them up in heaven!

This year, something wonderful happened to me a few days before the Easter holidays. My parents told me that my mum had to go to Romania for two weeks and my sister and I could go with her if we wanted to. You can't even imagine how delighted I was when I heard my parents finish that sentence! I wouldn't stop jumping up and down and I practically started crying with cheerfulness since I hadn't been to Romania ever since I left it nearly three years ago, when I was eight and a half years old. The only thing that saddened me a bit was losing my mobile a few days before leaving. Luckily, I was positive enough to forget about that and look at the bright side of things. On the day of our flight, I woke up extremely early because I was so excited. A few hours later, we got on the plane and after a while that day, we finally landed in the airport in Bucharest, the capital city. You probably know some things about Romania already, for example, the alleged "Dracula", who lived in the province Transylvania, or the way Romania is famous for its wine. Anyway, continuing on with the story, my granddad (on my dad's side) picked us up in his car and brought us back to Ploiesti, where I was born and used to live. He took us to our other grandparents (on my mum's side) where we were to stay for the rest of our visit.

While we were in Romania, I got a chance to visit all my old classmates from school. You wouldn't believe how happy I was to see them! I got to stay with them for the whole day and luckily, they had no classes that day so they had a party instead I also got to see my previous best friend and I went to her house a few times during my stay. It was also really lovely to see all my relatives, too, especially my grandparents and auntie. I got to go to many places and do a lot of things, as well. It was wonderful!

However, the time to leave arrived sooner than expected, but we had no choice. It was awfully depressing having to depart so soon. I didn't really want to leave because all my memories that I made there had to be abandoned again. Nevertheless, a few hours later, our plane landed back here, in Dublin airport. It was lovely coming back, but I still missed my relatives and friends. But as I said earlier on, I had to look at the bright side of things and forget about it. Also, my granny came over this summer so I got to see her really soon!

Unfortunately, all things have to come to an end, including this letter. I wrote to you some of the things that have happened this year, but not all of them. You'll probably get thousands more letters telling you about different things, but I thought you'd like to hear about these as well. Hope you enjoyed reading my letter as much as I enjoyed writing it! Please reply soon!

From your pen pal,
Stephany Stroiescu,
Scoil Realt Na Mara,
Skerries,
Co. Dublin.

Dear Grace:

A lot has happened down on this earth that is now without the happiness of you. Hopefully you are in the place more beautiful than the stars that twinkle in the sky. The place we know in this world as Heaven. Well, I think I should tell you about the news this year.

In March we had the war in Iraq. The war killing innocent Iraqis. The war George Bush said was good for the Iraqi people. And in the end, they didn't get the person they wanted, Saddam Hussein. And the war was all over Iraq having weapons of mass destruction. Many innocent people died and Grace if it was my choice, this war would not have gone ahead.

Early in the year was the space shuttle disaster. Columbia exploded at seven times the speed of sound. All seven on board died. One of the victims Illan Ramod was the first Israeli in space. I also wish this didn't happen Grace but unlike Iraq, nothing could be done about this catastrophe.

In June Ireland held the Special Olympics. It was the biggest event ever to be held in Ireland. A total of twenty-six countries took part. There were a lot of events including track and field, basketball, soccer, swimming, etc. The opening and closing ceremonies were held in Croke Park. The famous Special Olympic say is, "let me win but if I cannot win let me be brave in the attempt". My hometown, Tralee was a host to El Salvador. I am happy about this Grace. Every Irish person should be proud that this event was held in the country of Ireland.

You may not be into football but I'll tell you about the Kerry football team this year. In the Munster semi final Kerry beat Tipperary on a score line of 0-25 to 1-10. In the Munster final we beat Limerick 1-11 to 0-9. We brushed aside Roscommon by five points in the last eight (1-21 to 3-10) but Tyrone beat us in the semi final. They fired over 0-13 to Kerry's mere 0-6. I didn't like this happening Grace but at least it's not a disaster.

Well for Eurovision we did a competition called, "You're a Star". And Mickey Harte won. He represented us in Eurovision and came 11th with 53 points with, "We've got the World Tonight". Turkey won with "Everyway that I can". They got 165 points. T.A.T.U. were second and the United Kingdom came last with the wooden spoon (no points). This was good, Grace, a great achievement for Ireland. They are automatically in the competition next year.

Every year in Tralee we have a festival in the last week of August. There are fun rides and horse racing, but the most famous event to take place is the Rose of Tralee. It is broadcast on Irish T.V. This year we had a new presenter, Ryan Tubridy. The winner was the Dublin Rose by the name of Orla Tobin. Her father was from Kerry a place called Duagh. The Kerry Rose was called Jessica Lyons. I went to the horse racing and it was brilliant. It's great fun Grace. I wish you got a chance to go to the Tralee Festival.

Well, a competition was on television this summer called Cabin Fever. The presenter was Derek Mooney. It started with twelve contestants. However the ship crashed and sunk. In the end the winner was Elaine Power from Waterford. They built a new ship and the contestants sailed around the country. As a prize Elaine won 100,000 euro. Marie Walsh was a contestant from Castleisland in Kerry. She came Fifth. A good programme overall, I'm sure you would have liked it Grace.

The biggest oil tanker in the world, Prestige, sunk off the coast of Spain early in the year. When it sank it spilled one billion litres of oil into the sea. It ruined a lot of wildlife and has polluted the Spanish coast. This was quite bad, but nothing could be done about this.

We also had an outbreak of a disease called SARS (Severe Acute Respitory Syndrome). It was horrific. Thousands of people in China died. On the news all the Chinese people were wearing gas masks. Chinese students were coming to Ireland. Luckily (to my knowledge anyway) there were no cases in Ireland. This was catastrophic but the main thing is we're all safe, hey Grace!

Your death was tragic and I wish it didn't happen but the reason I speak to you about death is the death on our roads. It has risen this year. The penalty points were introduced in last October and they started well. Sixty-seven lives were saved in the first 6 months of penalty points. But this year, 14 people have already died on Kerry roads. Last year only 7 died so I think the penalty points were good but the deaths have risen. Something really has to be done. What do you think Grace?

Well to round up the news I'll tell you about the Bali bombing. In late last year a bomb exploded in the Sari nightclub in the island of Bali off the coast of Malaysia. About 100 died and about 180 were injured in the blast. About 33 British were among the dead people. People died from twelve different countries. Three Irish men were feared among the dead but were found. Their names were Mike Beatty, 25 from Limerick, Liam Mooney, 24 from Kilkenny and I'm not sure of the other man's name but he is safe as well. I hope the dead are up with you. Australia and Malaysia believe the Al-Qaead terrorist group were responsible. Bali was called the "Island of Paradise". I just hope the victims are in a new paradise, a paradise which I hope you are also in. This was a disaster Grace, it shows the world's cruel side.

In March my cousins from America and England came. Their names were (from England) Hugh, Joie, Poppy and Jack. And Michael, Dori, Nicky and Noelana came from America. They stayed for six days and then a day later Tim Elaine and Josh came from England. We all had great fun. On the last day we played a big soccer match in a soccer hall. My team won on penalties. I got a nice surprise. Josh told me he was staying for another two days. I got sick the day they left. I was sad but it's not the end of the world.

My hobbies include football, soccer, swimming, hurling, running, reading and a whole lot more. I play football with Ballymac U-12. I like all kinds of sport. On Friday I'm running in a 1500 metre race. The top 10 get medals so I have a chance but I'm really nervous.

My name is Kevin Sweeney. I am 12 years old born on July the 30th 1991. I have black hair and blue-green eyes. I have glasses, as my sight is 3.75. My Mom is Sheila and my Dad is Mike. I have one sister called Emma and my twin brothers Michael and Luke. (They're ten and they are rascals). Well I'd love to go on about that but I can't because it might put you off. I go to O'Brennan National School and I'm in 6th class. I'm going into secondary next year. Well Grace there's my fact file now I'll tell you where I live.

I live in a place called Ballinorig about two miles outside of Tralee. I live in an area of about a square kilometre with about 17 houses and another two going up but it is not an estate it's in the country. My house is in a land area of about an acre. It is a 5-bedroomed detached house with four lawns all around the same size. We also own a pre school. The house itself is 15 years old and the Pre School four. It's surrounded by trees, ditches and hedges. The house is painted white and that's the info of the house.

In June I went on holiday to Majorca. We stayed in the Habitat Apartments near a town called Puerto Pollensa in the north of the island. The temperatures were hot. It was the hottest summer in the biggest Balearic Island for 138 years. Once the temperature was 41 degrees Celsius. Well in the swimming pool I learned how to dive. The deep end was 2 metres 20. It was an amazing experience when I swam in the Mediterranean Sea. The water was so warm compared to the freezing beaches of Ireland. We stayed for twelve days. We got back on June 29th at 2.30am. I enjoyed the rest of my summer holiday but that was the highlight of it.

In the past year my brother Luke (yeah one of the rascals) developed a condition called epilepsy. Epilepsy is when you get seizures. Seizures are abnormal electrical activity in the brain causing him to drop unconscious. He has had six of them and I've seen four (they're pretty scary) and Michael has seen five. He takes tablets called Epilim two times a day. Four days ago it was a year since he had a seizure. So his condition is under control.

Well Grace when you so tragically died you left many who loved you behind. But I hope and I know that they will join you some day. And I know that you are a golden angel in God's presence. I hope I will get the honour of meeting you. For now, goodbye my special friend, my special dear Grace.

Kind Regards

Kevin Sweeney,
O'Brennan's N.S.,
Kielduff,
Tralee,
Co. Kerry.

Dear Grace:

Life, my friend, is a wonderful thing,
It's something we must take with pride.
There is so much in life that we can fulfil,
As long as we don't try to hide.
If you make life a chore,
It will turn out a bore,
So why make life harder for you?
Have fun in the sun,
Don't complain in the rain,
Just go and find something to do.
Life can be good crack,
Just give it a whack,
And try not to get all upset,
Live life to the max, Just try to relax,
Be happy and try not to fret.
Don't let life pass you by,
But don't try to die
Because Heaven will take you in time.
Make up with your foes,
Attend parties and shows,
Because friendship is far from a crime.
One day we will go,
To a place no-one knows,
And stay there in eternal rest.
So respect what you've got,
And let life play it's plot,
Until god gives us life at it's best.

So this is the end of my poetic trend,
I hope you enjoyed it like me.
I'll see you one day,
In a life long and gay,
Don't forget to call in for some tea.

Jodi Cox, St. Brigid's National School, Greystones

Dear Grace:

As I know nothing of the secrets of death, I cannot express to you my sympathy, but I know you have gone on to a better life through the mystic veils of the clouds. You are probably aware of all that has been happening here on earth from your seat in the Top Box, which is where I am sure you are. I sometimes feel certain that I have seen the sunlight gilding the top of your head from behind a cloud as it drifted across the balmy blue sky.

As the darkness of the dying year faded, I watched the golden dawning of the year 2003 from my bedroom window. We had no snow, no ice and therefore no reasons to stay home from school. By the middle of January, the days were growing longer and milder. My long-awaited holiday was looming nearer. At home, we bought a new car, the Mondeo Zetec. We are all very happy with it, especially Dad, who needs a reliable car to take him in and out of work. It also brought us to Dublin, to the R.D.S., where my sister was taking part in the Young Scientist & Technology Exhibition 2002-2003 with her friend Rebecca Curtin. They won two prizes, a Best Display award and a Highly Recommended award. They will be taking part again this year.

January faded slowly into February and our skiing holiday was drawing very close. On the morning of the 14th my mother drove us to Kent station where we waited excitedly for the train that would take us to Dublin. Upon leaving the train we met our uncle, who was accompanying us to Andorra. We got on a plane that took us away from Ireland and to our destination, Toulouse. We then collected our baggage and embarked on a four hour-long bus journey that would end up at the heart of the Pyrenees. The next morning we went up to the mountain in a creaky, rocky cable car, but the noise could not drown out the cheery, excited chat that filled the cramped, slightly damp lift. When we reached the top of the mountain we rented our skis, boots, goggles and for some "unknown" reason, Dad bought me a helmet (as if I'd ever do anything dangerous). We clipped our skis and set off down the mountain. At eleven o'clock we went to ski-class and then in the afternoon we went off on our own to try out some of the skills we had learned in the morning class. That evening we went for a relaxing Jacuzzi, and afterwards a friendly game of bowling. It continued in this enjoyable vein over the course of the next few days. Finally, on the last day of the holiday we were forced to pack our clothes, which had been strewn over a vast area considering we were only there for a week. We went to bed that night sad that our holiday was over, but having had a great time all the same.

Valentines Day came and went with no arrows from Cupid raining down on me, but I am sure the air is filled with the sound of whistling arrows shooting your way. In March, the football season was drawing to a close, with Manchester United unfortunately dominating the Premiership and European giants winning all round them in the Champions League. Meanwhile, in school, the teachers were keeping our noses hard to the grindstone with upcoming Communion, Confirmation, Drumcondra and entrance exams looming. But the discovery of a new sport, pitch and putt had wrought a change in my pastime. I now spent as much time as realistically possible at the Brinny Pitch & Putt Club with my friends and tried not to think of the dredged hours I spent in the classroom with the unrelenting teacher. The weather became warmer and brought with it a new television programme, You're a Star, which would, by public vote, choose our Eurovision contestant. Micky Joe Harte emerged from it victorious but unfortunately did not win a prize in the Eurovision, where Turkey beat all opponents to claim top prize. We did manage to secure a place in next year's Eurovision, so it was not a complete loss after all.

March merged its way slowly into April, not fast enough for me though because of the prospect of a two-week Easter break, with Easter eggs to boot. Finally, the holiday came and the lead-up to Easter Sunday was as enjoyable as always, playing with friends, counting Easter eggs (always essential) and enjoying time-off with my family. On Easter Saturday night we went to Mass as usual, then afterwards we were allowed to eat one of our Easter Eggs Galaxy for me as is our yearly tradition. That night, we went to bed with our tummies full of excitement (and chocolate). After a rushed dinner the next day we raced up the stairs to grab another Easter Egg and start eating again. All too soon the holidays were drawing to a close, and the school year was recommencing and the teachers were working us harder than ever before to ensure that we lived up to our full potential. By the end of May, I had all my clothes and personal effects packed, and I was ready to set off once more to sunnier lands.

On the 1st of June we boarded the plane headed for Portugal, with a mingled feeling of jubilation and tiredness. It had been another early morning. The flight took less than three hours, enough time for my excitement levels to mount. But as we entered the airport we saw a lot of commotion by the baggage claim. Sure enough, when we got nearer, the conveyor belt was rolling devoid of all baggage. My excitement seeped away as fast as it had come.

After the chaos of the lost baggage had subsided (they had been transferred to a commercial flight to Lisbon) and all articles accounted for, we were off on another stuffy, airless ride on a bus. We were left off at Jardim de Vau in the Algarve, where we were to take up residence for the next two weeks. When we got our second level apartment, we unpacked our clothes and flung on our swimming togs, then headed down to the beach to catch some of the evening sun that bathed the seaside with dappled golden light. That night, we rounded off the evening with a drink in the bar, and a game of snooker while we listened to the soothing music that was played live in the bar nightly. When we left the bar and trudged up the stairs we all fell into bed and fell fast asleep immediately.

The next three days passed lazily, whether we were swimming in the pool or the sea, soaking up the sun on the beach or playing on the grass next to the apartment it didn't matter, we were always having a memorable time. We had a trip to Slide and Splash, a nearby waterpark, planned for Thursday, so we awoke early that morning to pack our gear, cameras and snacks to keep us going. When we got there our hopes were not dashed, slides that wound around each other in never ending circles were separated by almost vertical chutes, from which screams emitted constantly. We deposited our bags and tried to decide which slide to begin with. We decided (against my sister's bidding) on one of the steep slides and it did not disappoint. In fact, none of the slides we tested before lunch disappointed. For lunch we had rolls with ham and chicken, and, without waiting the required hour to avoid cramps, set out again. By the end of the day we were exhausted and each slide had been so thoroughly canvassed that we decided to pack our things and wait for the homebound bus. We savoured the thought of a restful, relaxing day on the beach that we were planning the next day.

And so the holiday went on with many other exciting day trips such as deep-sea fishing and a trip to the gypsy market. On the last day of the holiday, we went down to the pool to have a final swim and to say goodbye to everybody we had met during the holiday. We went to bed early that night after packing as we were expected to get up at two in the morning the next day. I slept the whole way through the bus journey back to Faro Airport and the plane trip home. Our luggage had mercifully not been lost on the return trip so we were able to collect all our belongings, and get back to normality.

Normality, however, was not going to last for long. The Special Olympics, for which Ireland had been preparing itself for the last few months, was finally bearing down on us. The opening ceremony was truly spectacular and the facilities the organisers had in place were second to none. The athletes took part in many sports and showed viewers that they too formed part of this world. Until we meet again, nine flights of clouds above, goodbye.

Joey Donovan,
Goggins Hill N.S.,
Ballinhassig,
Co. Cork.

Dear Grace:

I CAN'T WAIT

When I am an old woman I shall wear a mini skirt,
And a red, blue, and yellow T-shirt with high leather boots.

I shall live on a farm and ride a cow instead of a horse,
And I will train my cats to rob AIB banks.
I'll pierce my eyebrow and dye my hair green,
And have a tattoo of a love heart on my arm.
I will paint my house bright, bright pink,
With a blue border and pictures of butterflies on it.
I will have long hair and put it in pig-tails,
And have long nails and red nail varnish.

My husband can be the sensible one for a change.
He'll have to wear a nice shirt instead of that
Disgraceful one he usually wears.
And he'll have to stop swearing.
And learn to cook once in a while.
I can't wait until I'm old.
Then I can do as I please.

Fiona Murphy, Scoil Maria Assumpta, Kerry

Dear Grace:

Its Elaine here just thought I'd write you this letter to let you know what's happening with the world these days! So, what's it like up in heaven? Is it true that you can't feel pain, and can you sit on clouds without falling though them? I'd love to know what it's like to be an angel! So much has happened since you've died, some good things and some bad things. I suppose you can't wait to hear them so I'll start straight away!

First the Twin Towers collapsed and Iraq and America went to war. It was a horrible experience and I suppose in a way you were kind of lucky not to be here experiencing it aswell.

Then there were the Special Olympics, which were held in Dublin (Ireland) for the very first time, it was the longest sporting event in the world this year. There was even a new aquatic centre built for it (I went there on my school tour, it's really good)! Speaking of school let me tell you about mine.

I go to Saint Kevin's G.N.S. (Girls National School). I'm in 6th class and my teachers name is MS. Ni Ghliasain. I'm in a class of thirty-six. My school uniform is navy with a cream shirt. It's actually really nice!

Did you have a mobile phone? They practically have new models out every week now! You can even take pictures with some of them! They used to be the size of bricks, now you can get them even smaller than your baby finger.

There are loads of new fashions out aswell and the eighties are back! There's baggy trousers with strings attached to them, netted hats tops with only one sleeve and loads more! I'd say the clothes you used to wear were a lot different than that!

Who was your favourite pop singer? I really like the RnB singers like Usher or Nelly, I also like Beyonce (she's got a really good voice). I don't really have a favourite pop band. How about you, Grace?

Did you like Barbies? If you did then you'd love these new dolls called Bratz! They're much more fashionable than Barbies! There are loads of other new toys out as well, from dolls than can walk, talk and cry to electronic drawing machines! They're really good (not to mention expensive)!

Did you have a favourite author? Mine is Jacqueline Wilson or R.L. Stine. I really like reading, that's probably because I do much of it in school.

By the way what school did you go to? And where did you live? (I didn't really get a chance to ask you many questions yet)! So, is it really packed up in heaven or do you all have your own sections? Oh, and do you have to clean and shine your halo everyday so it doesn't go rusty? And do you always have to wear white? Where would you have liked to go to college? And what would you have liked to be when you were older? I'd love to be either a fashion designer or an author then again I'd also like to be an actress. Do you think I could be the next Julia Roberts!!!

I'd also like to be President / Taoiseach so I could make loads of rules like everything is free in shops on weekends or no homework for pupils over ten! (I don't think that will ever happen though)!

What would you wish for if you had three wishes? The first thing I'd wish for would probably be for everything to be made of chocolate! Then I'd wish for no more war or poverty, and for my third wish, I'd wish for three more wishes!!!

And what would you do if you won the lotto? I really don't know what I'd do with it!

Do you remember your first day at school? My teacher was sick and I had a substitute called Mrs McNamara, I could never say her name so I called her Mrs McBanana! I was four when I started school and I remember walking into the classroom and seeing crayons and bricks and pages all set out on the table. I was so shocked to see so many children all in the same room!

Who was your best friend? I've got loads of friends but I don't really know whom my best one is!

How many brothers and sisters had you got or did you have any? I've got one brother and three sisters. (I'm the youngest)! I've also got a little niece called Lauren who is one and one half.

There is now a big metal pole in Dublin's City Centre called the Spire, it's about 150 metres high and it cost about four million euro to build!

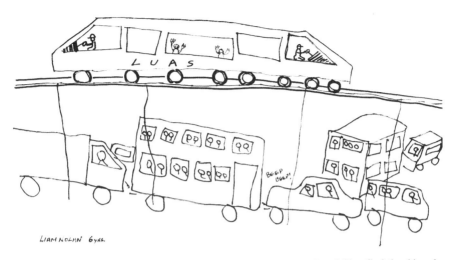

LIAM NOLAN 6yrs.

There's also a new train being built called the Luas. It should be finished by the year 2005 but we really don't know for sure.

Also over the past year people have been investigating a disease called SARS, short for Severe Acute Respiratory Syndrome. Loads of people have died from it and it is quite serious. Luckily enough it never came to Ireland. You'll also be glad to know there is now a cure for HHT and many lives have been saved.

In America, at the moment, there is a hurricane going on called Isabel. Nobody has died from it yet but it is getting stronger and stronger. Some people have even moved to different parts of the country to get away from it.

Also, on cigarette boxes, they are beginning to put photographs of lungs and other parts of the body, which get damaged by smoke on them to try and stop people from smoking.

They are also putting tax on chewing gum because so many people just throw it on the ground and there is already tax on plastic bags for the same reason. Do you think this is a good idea, Grace?

Where was the last place you went on holidays? I'm going to Wales in October for ten days, and just a few months ago I went to Wexford for a week. Even though I didn't go far I really enjoyed it, especially the beach!

Have you ever been on a plane? You probably have but I've only ever been on one once and that was when I went to Belgium. That was probably my favourite holiday.

Do you usually watch the Eurovision? This year it was in May and Turkey won. Ireland didn't even come close, but I thought we were really good! A singer called Micky Joe Harte represented Ireland and he sang a song called "We've got the world tonight!" There's even a new programme out called "You're a Star" and it's where a group of judges get together and decide who will sing for Ireland at the song contest.

What was your favourite TV programme? There are loads of new cartoons out now, and did you watch Coronation Street or Eastenders? There's loads of brilliant new storylines in them as well!

I can't wait for Hallowe'en! It's only a few more weeks away and I'm really excited! Do you normally dress up and go trick or treating? If you did what did you dress up as last time? Me and my friend both dressed up as twins and had signs around our necks saying "Terrible Twins!" We did look kind of funny! I also really like looking at the fireworks and bonfires but I really hate bangers. I think everybody's favourite part of Halloween is all the sweets! I go around to about three roads and I get about two bags full!

Have you seen the new euro money? It's a lot nicer than pounds. The one-cent, two-cent and five-cent are bronze, the 10c, 20c and 50c are gold and the one euro and two euro are silver and gold. The notes are a lot nicer as well. It was all introduced on 1st of January 2001. All the countries in Europe are using it except that each country has a different picture on the back. The Irish coins have harps on them. On the notes there are all different pictures and there are all different colours as well. The five euro notes are blue, the twenties are bluish green, fifties are orange, one hundred euro notes are green, the two hundreds are yellow and the five hundreds are purple.

What was your favourite season? Mine would probably be summer. But it's autumn now and all the leaves are covering the ground gradually. It's also getting a lot colder and the wasps and bees are beginning to die. All the birds are migrating for the winter and the squirrels and hedgehogs are going into hibernation.

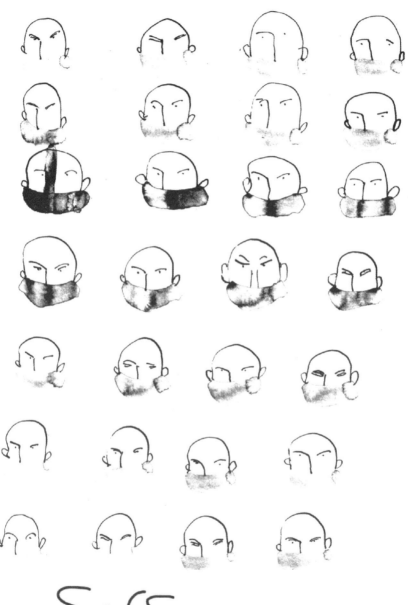

Sars

Well, Grace I suppose I've come to the end of this letter, but hopefully I'll talk to you again soon. Just remember everyone down here on earth really misses you and we'll always remember you.

From your good friend

Elaine O'Carroll,
St. Kevin's G.N.S.,
Tallaght,
Dublin

P.S. Sorry if this letter is a bit late, but I wasn't sure if your new address was:

>Heaven 17
>Cloud   7
>H.24
>Or if you were on cloud nine.

Dear Grace:

And now I come to say goodbye,
And let you fly back to the sky,
Where dainty cherubs learn to sing,
And angels try to earn their wings.

Where God sits in his heavenly towers,
And angels marvel at his powers,
I'd rather sleep in the clouds and spires,
Than down in the dungeons, blackened by fires.

Zoe McGaley

Dear Grace:

My name is Lisa Dempsey and my birthday is the 22nd of August. I just had my eleventh birthday. I'm really sorry you died. It must have been really hard for your parents and your whole family. I feel extra sorry for your dad since you died in his arms. It was really sad because you were so young and you could have seen lots of good things that have happened. The only down side was that you would have seen lots of bad things as well.

My family is made up of four people. My mum, my dad, my brother and myself:

My mum used to work in the Bank of Ireland, but now she studies Homeopathy. She is in her fourth year of learning Homeopathy. She also does reflexology. Reflexology is carried out on the feet. It is believed that every organ, such as the kidneys, is mapped in miniature on your feet and by pressing on the feet, you can help someone feel better.

During the summer my mum studied the 'Axelson method'. This involves a series of exercises and massage to help children or adults with dyslexia, among other conditions. Dyslexia is where some adults or children have a mental block to recognising word and letter patterns. Last year the government set up a special task force to look into ways of recognising and helping people with this condition.

My dad is a member of the Garda Siochana. He will be 21 years in the force this year. My dad was born in Galway, which as you know, is on the West coast of Ireland. He used to go to Aran when he was growing up, and he likes to go back there every now and again. My dad does all sorts of police work but he is especially involved in helping women who have been hurt by domestic violence. My dad has just finished doing a course at the University of Teesside in England and hopes to get his Masters qualification in "Justice and Society."

My dad also goes to Lourdes every year. He has been going there every September for as long as I can remember. He helps people who are seriously sick and disabled and who need to be pushed by wheelchair.

My brother is called Christopher and he is going to be fifteen in February. He goes to Grammar School in Dundalk. He is supposed to do two hours of studying every day. The special subjects he chose to do are Woodwork and

Technical Graphics.

He likes to go on the Internet. He also likes to play computer games. He has lots of computer games like Tiberian Sun and Command and Conquer. He likes to read books. His favourite is Tom Clancy. Tom Clancy writes books about secret agents.

My auntie, who lives in Italy, had a baby called Eanna May Alfonso. She is about four months old. She was born in May. She came over to visit us in August this year from her home in Italy. She had a christening in Galway while she was in Ireland. After the christening we went to an Italian restaurant with all my aunts, uncles and cousins. It was great fun. I had Penne Polo, which is my favourite food.

I know you are probably tired of hearing about my family, but I would like to tell you just one more thing about them. My grandfather died last year in September of a heart attack while he was at mass. It was a big shock to us all. My dad and granny were away in Lourdes, in France when it happened. They had only been in Lourdes one night and had to get the next flight home. He was not very old; He was just seventy years of age. We were glad we had given him a surprise party back in March for his birthday. We pretended that the party was for my auntie Colette so my granddad got a big shock when he finally realised it was really for him. My uncle did a "This is your life" speech for him and told us lots of funny stories about my granddad.

Now that I have told you all about my family, let me tell you some of the things that have been happening since you have been gone.

There was a terrorist attack on 11th September 2001. Two planes flown by Middle Eastern terrorists flew them into two buildings called the Twin Towers. Over three thousand people were killed as well as the terrorists themselves. The Twin Towers ended up going on fire. People jumped out of the windows and eventually the towers collapsed. There was a lot of commotion and fire fighters were called to the rescue. The whole of New York came to a stand still. People were panicking because they did not know whether their family members were alive or dead. People in Ireland and around the world, were very worried because there is a huge amount of foreigners working in New York City. A few weeks after the attack, there were prayers at the site for all that died. It was very moving to see some children on TV reading prayers for their fathers who were fire fighters and who had died on that terrible day. In Ireland, we held a national day of mourning for the victims and their families.

This event lead to a war in the Middle East to try and get rid of a man called Saddam Hussein. Some people think that bombing the Twin Towers was an excuse to take control of the oilrigs, as this would push oil prices up very high and give control to America.

While Astrologists were studying the stars last year, they noticed an asteroid heading towards Earth. It was supposed to hit Earth in nine years time but luckily, it has gone off course.

We were very lucky to be able to see Mars, the planet, in the sky at night with the naked eye. It was in the North direction near the moon. This happened in August around my birthday. It looked like a big round red star.

Last year, when I was in Spain on my summer holidays, Ireland was playing in the World Cup. We got off to a brilliant start. We were staying in a resort in Fuerteventura, which is an Island off Spain. We travelled by boat to Lanzarote, to meet with my uncle, aunt and cousins. When we were there we went to an Irish pub to watch one of the Ireland matches. The atmosphere was great fun, everyone was shouting at the television and they went really mad when Ireland won. Everyone was shouting, singing and dancing on the streets; all the cars were beeping their horns. I was sorry we had to leave for the boat back to Fuerteventura.

I met a new friend while I was on holidays. Her name is Kim Sheppard and she lives in England. She has a little brother called Mark. We swam and played pool most of the days in the sunshine and at night there was entertainment such as music and competitions in the hotel. In the morning, around nine o'clock, there was a huge wake up call from seven dwarfs singing "Hi Ho." It was a great holiday and I hope to go there again some day.

Last September, there was a Peace Conference in Darver Castle in Knockbridge. Six Elders of various Native American Tribes came over to tell us stories and ways to make peace. 'Momfeather' was the Chief Elder of the Cherokee Indians. She was my favourite because she was like a grandmother who told lots of children's stories. She also gave me a book that she wrote herself filled with Cherokee Legends. She is married to Dean who was with her. Leon was the Elder and President of the Navajo Nation in New Mexico. He knows a lot about the stars and what will happen in the future. He travels the world talking about how to save our planet from destruction. Another of my favourites was Cynthia Walker who is a founder member of Grandmothers of Mother Earth. At the Conference she talked about the Mayan Prophecies and also explained to us how the Mayan Calendar worked. She was very

interesting. Laura Shurts uses ancient ways to help people over their fears. Warren Ramey is a teacher of the old ways the use of the old medicine ways of his past traditions. He had a lovely walking stick, which was made from some wood that fell in a lightening storm. On the top for the handle, his friend carved out a bear. Also last but not least, Margaret Connolly, who is the Irish Elder of the Celtic Ways, hosted the conference. My headmaster's sister sang an ancient song of Brigid. Her name is Padraigin Ni Uallachain. She will soon have a new book coming out about the old stories of County Louth.

Centuries ago, Queen Meave married Aihill the King in Connaught. They fought one night over their belongings and Meave realised that the King had one bull more that her. She knew of a similar bull in Ulster and gathered up an army to go and steal it. Cuchulainn, who used to be called Setanta, is associated with Knockbridge. He protected Ulster and fought off Meave's men. She still managed to steal the bull.

A few weeks ago, the local football team in Cooley arranged for a big bull to be made by handicapped children and designed by a local artist Paul O'Hare, they took the bull to Tulsk in Roscommon and walked the ancient journey of the "Táin" back to Cooley and returned the bull to the people of the area. This raised funds for a charity but also helped reverse the old story. The members of Retrieve Foundation, who worked for peace on the land, handed over three gifts to the walkers. These were, an ancient map of Ireland which was in the shape of a bull when put on it's side, a flag showing the ancient symbol of wisdom, compassion and understanding, and I was asked to give the candle of peace.

The Candle of Peace was lit from a candle, which originally started in The Hague in Brussels and has travelled the world.

I'm really glad I got this chance to write to you because it has given me an opportunity to tell you what has happened over the past year that is important to me. I hope you have found my letter interesting and informative. I enjoyed writing it very much. I hope you are happy where you are and if you see my granddad, please say hello to him for my family and me and give him a great big hug.

Lots of love,
Lisa Dempsey,
St. Mary's N.S.,
Knockbridge, Dundalk, Co. Louth.

Dear Grace:

How are you doing? Do you like wherever you are? I hope you do. Have you read the book with the extracts from the letters that children have sent you? I have heard some of it. From what I heard your friends and family miss you and love you dearly. What I heard made it clear that everybody cared for you more than anyone could have guessed or imagined. Your death has affected so many people, whether they knew you or not. I can tell you truthfully that when I heard your story I was greatly troubled and disturbed, that someone so young and with so much to live for should die so soon. You have missed so much that you should have been able to see, experience, enjoy, face and sometimes even despair and worry over. I hope you are happy and content wherever you may be, for it would pain me to know or even think that you are sad and unhappy.

I wish I had had the honour to meet you when you were alive just like many others have, as you could have taught us so much, you could have opened our eyes to the pain and suffering in the world a lot sooner, which would have made a difference, a big difference and it is a difference to be thought about and you Grace, you have made me think about so much, and all this, is from your short lifetime.

What are your friends like Grace? Mine are great. Are all your friends girls? Mine aren't, some of them are boys but not a lot of them. I'm not in the same class as my school friends anymore. The school board said we had too many teachers in our school so all the classes got split up and no one is with their friends. I hate it but my new class is O.K. I've made new friends there. They're great as well.

Do you like your parents Grace? Mine are lovely. They help me with everything I need help with. I'm sure your parents are great too. From what I've heard they adored and cherished you. You must love them very much, just like they love you. I know I would, as would anyone else. I was told that you died in your father's arms. That must have been very painful for him. Your death must have been very painful for your whole family to go through. Their grief was probably beyond my comprehension.

Do you know all your grandparents? I didn't. My Grandfather died before I was born. My dad told me he would have been proud of me. I hope your grandparents are proud of you, but of course they are. How could they not be? My Grandmothers are great I couldn't live without them.

Do you have any hobbies Grace? I do. I love swimming, reading and playing the fiddle. I read the fifth Harry Potter book in two days. My friends couldn't believe it. Every Wednesday I have fiddle lessons in my school. I've been doing it for about a year now. The teacher is really nice. I also swim on a competitive swimming team, three hours a week every week. I like astronomy Grace. Do you? I like to know about the constellations, the stars, the moon they're all beautiful.

Do you like school? I don't, it's so boring. I sometimes already know about what the teacher is teaching us. What's your teacher like? Mine's strict but she's a very good teacher in general. I learn a lot from her and she seems to like me. My classmates hate her but that's their opinion. I'd love to study psychology; it's so interesting to look into the depths of human emotions, hate, love, joy, sorrow they're all so fascinating. Do you have anything you want to study? Do you have ambitions? Any dreams you want to fulfill? I sure hope so. Everybody should have a dream, a desire. It's part of human nature.

Have you seen what's been going on this year? Some of the things that have happened have been terrible and very sorrowful while some have been good.

A lot has happened this year, the war on Iraq for one. It was devastating and very upsetting to see so many people injured or killed, don't you think? It's something that most people wish had never, ever happened just like many other things in the world today but this, this was avoidable. They could have stopped it; those innocent people did not need to die. The war is over now but it will stay on in our memories and in our hearts for a very long time, most probably it will never leave us. I hope nothing like it happens in the future but all we can do is hope that people have learned their lessons, which they probably haven't. What do you think about it all?

Did you know that a 20 year old UWE student was arrested for letting loose a potentially crippling computer virus? If a computer was infected every Microsoft Word Document on the host computer would have an 'L' added on to the end of any world that ends in a vowel. This would make millions of letters, contracts, statements and manuscripts all over the world unreadable to the majority of the population. That would be devastating for a lot of people but I think it would be kinda cool but I guess my opinion is only one of many. What about you - what's your opinion?

The Special Olympics were on this year. It was amazing! Nations from all over the world came together to join in on the games. I was watching the

opening ceremony were you? I thought it was wonderful, all the fireworks and the dancers, it took my breath away. After that the games took place for a week. Their motto was "let me win, but, if I cannot win, let me brave in the attempt". I thought that was very deep and very meaningful because it applies to everyone. Everyone deserves a chance to shine. The athletes were so happy when they were competing. I couldn't help but smile. I was at the Global Youth Summit that was on MTV about the Special Olympics. We talked about what it's like to be physically or mentally disabled and how disabled people have feelings too, how they should be treated right. I totally agree with that, we have to treat fellow human beings with respect and compassion, what do you think? Eunice Kennedy Shriver had a vision to bring us all together and it's great...it's brilliant. I hope you were there to watch it just like the rest of us. It was truly spectacular. Nobody should have missed it.

J.K. Rowling's new book 'Harry Potter and the Order of the Phoenix' came out this June. It was really cool. Thousands of people lined up to get the book at midnight. I wasn't allowed because my mum and dad were going out, but I got the book the next morning so it was O.K. I absolutely love Harry Potter. Have you read any of the Harry Potter books? I hope you did. They are really amazing books. I find they kind of...pull you in, make you feel like you're there, like you're part of the magical world they're set in. But now that I think about it, maybe that's just me. Do you have books where you are? I hope you do. Stories, myths, legends are part of almost every culture in every part of the world. It would be a shame if you or anyone else for that matter were deprived of them.

The new 'Lord of the Rings' movie is coming out in December. I don't suppose you got a chance to see any of them, then again maybe you did. J.R.R. Tolkien was a genius to write a masterpiece, such as Lord of the Rings, the detail in them is so rich, the emotion in them feels so real and the passion behind them is just...just amazing. I hope you have read or seen them. They're brilliant but then again you might not like that sort of thing.

Roddy Doyle's play "The Woman Who Walked Into Doors" was in the Helix this year. I wasn't allowed go and see it because I was too young. The same play is also on at a Theatre Festival. I don't know much about the festival but I read a little bit about it, it sounds cool.

I'm sorry you have to miss all of these things, even the bad things, no one should.

Dear Grace you are a great loss to this world and your memory will be honoured. Dear Grace we will never forget you. I didn't know you Grace and I never will but I think you should never have died. I hope that you can read this because it was written for you. I hope you find something, anything good from these words.

Yours Ever,
Emma-Louise Hutchinson,
Holy Child Senior N.S.,
Whitehall,
Dublin.

Dear Grace
Letter Writers of the Future

We received some wonderful letters from seven year old children attending Scoil Naomh Eirc, Kilmoyley, Ard Fhearta, Co Kerry.

Because the competition, at this time, is only open to 5th & 6th Class, your entries did not qualify.However I would like to acknowledge your effort, and congratulate your teacher, Eilin Loibhead. You have a very talented group of children and the Grace Nolan Foundation will be sending you a little gift, so to all of you, well done.

The next two pages to are two edited letters from two very inquisitive seven year old children.......

Warmest Regards,
Mike Nolan.

Dear Grace:

How are you ? I hope you are safe and happy. When I see nature I think heaven is very close to us and I don't believe you' re very far away at all !

Most Children who write to you are in 5th and 6th class Grace - I'm in 2nd class! instead of telling you about the changes in the world Grace, I'd like to tell you about my friends, my school and myself.

I like using the computer, I can use power point and make slide shows. I have a donkey, a rabbit, a cat and a dog. Well, I used to have a cat, actually I used to have two cats, but they got lost. I like throwing the ball for my dog; his name is Clint, after the actor Clint Eastwood.

While I was on holiday with my family in Mayo, we heard on the news, that the planet Mars would be very close to Earth. We were all looking for it everywhere and then we saw it, it was absolutely beautiful ! Do you see the stars and planets from heaven Grace?

Grace, I've been wondering about heaven. Do Angels take people to heaven or is there a special machine or something to get you there ? Do you enjoy heaven or is it boring ? What do you do all day and what is it really like ? Do you just sit there or do you have fun ? What can you play and are there fair grounds ? Are there animals and shops ? Are there swimming pools and schools ? Are there computers and toys ? Are there towns, is there a sea ? Is heaven under ground or is it way up in the sky ? Do you meet God or is he working all the time ? If you meet my great granny Sarah Carroll, will you say that I said HELLO ! Is there something on earth that isn't in heaven ? Hope you say no ! Do people speak a different language in heaven ? You must be exhausted by all my questions Grace !

I hope you liked my letter and I hope to get a chance to write to you again.

Love from

Clare Jennifer Breen

Dear Grace:

How are you, I live in a place called Dineens in Co Kerry. I am a twin ! I have a twin brother called Padraig, we were born on 14th February, Yes ! That's valentines day. We live on a farm, its a busy place and there always something to do.
Last year we did a project all about trees in school, I wrote a poem Grace, here it is...

> Spring I dress in green,
> Summer I dance in the sun,
> Autumn winds leave me bare
> Winter I stand and stare,
> This is my life, year in, year out,
> How lovely, I'm a tree.

What do you think of it Grace ? Do you like poems ? Do you like trees and nature ?
I like trees, they are planted in my area, to shelter our homes, animals and fields. Trees also decorate our gardens and countryside.
Trees provide food and homes for the animals and birds. We have apple trees, blackcurrant trees and gooseberry trees and every Christmas my family chooses a growing Christmas tree and we plant it in our garden. We also get grandad a tree, one of grandads big trees blew down last year and now we are using it for the fire.
Last year we did a project called "Dissolving Boundaries, and our partner school is in Derry. The children there described what it was like living in Derry city, it sounded very different to living in Kilmoyley ! The children had lovely accents.
We won a competition about the environment and the prize was a trip to visit the ship Celtic Explorer in Galway Bay. Another bus trip !
We went on a school tour to Crag Caves, were you ever in a cave Grace ? When you go into the cave first, it feels cold, but you get used to it, then you can see funny shapes in the stalactites and stalagmites, a bit like making shapes out of clouds. Do you float on a cloud Grace ?

Grace can i ask you some Questions ?
Is there a school in Heaven ?
What do you do in heaven ?
Do you go to the shops ?
Can you eat and drink ?
Is there a swimming pool in heaven ?
Is there ploughing matches in heaven ?
Before I go Grace, I'd like to tell you that I saw your photograph on the cover of last years book. You Look Beautiful, actually you look very like my aunt Patricia.

Bye for now Grace,
Keep smiling
From Maura Godley

About Grace ...

A lot of children have asked to know a little bit more about Grace, so let me tell you.............

Grace Julia Nolan was born on June 23rd 1990 in Cork, and like all children, she was special.

It was also a wonderful time to be in Ireland, because Grace was born during World Cup Italia 90', when Irish eyes were smiling and the nation was boiling over with soccer fever.My wife June had given birth to our second child, another girl and new sister for our 2 year old daughter Aimee to play with.It was a time of high emotion and I was floating to the nearest toy shop where I purchased a giant yellow teddy bear draped in the Irish colours.I returned to the hospital, plonked the teddy bear on Junes bed, and said "Now, isn't she lovely !

June frowned, I had bounced teddy Cascarino to hard on the bed & disturbed rest time. Another frown, "No not him," I said, "Grace, its Grace who is lovely".It was not surprising as she got older that Graces favourite colour was yellow, it was hard for her to see anything else, she was five by the time she reached to the height of the bear.

Two days later Ireland beat Romania in a penalty shoot out to reach the quarter finals of the world cup, what a week !

Over the next nine years Grace developed into a real funny personality with a great sense of humour, Grace was very popular in school and she loved having fancy dress parties where she would invite all her classmates and more.Grace loved going to school and attended Scoil Bhride, Eglantine on the Douglas Road, Cork. Her hobbies were ballet and swimming, she really enjoyed Art and won several art competitions.In general she liked to dress up and become one of her favourite Disney characters like Jasmine and Ariel.It was an all year event through Christmas, Easter and Halloween.

Graces favourite holiday destination was Portugal, it was heaven on earth to her, swimming all day and making new friends every year.

I almost forgot to tell you, Grace loved all animals, even insects, spiders & worms, her favourite animals would have been horses, followed by Cats and dogs.

When Grace made her communion she was not very well, but she was determined to be there with her classmates and teachers, it was one of the happiest days in her short life, dressed like an angel, singing the hymns.Her favourite Hymn was "The Queen of the may."

surrounded by her family she was queen of the day .

Grace has three sisters, Aimee, Eva, and Julia and three brothers Ryan, Dean and Michael who all miss very much, along with her mum and of course me, Graces Dad.

Well I hope I have answered some of your questions for now, keep writing and I hope you enjoyed this years book !

Warmest Regards Mike Nolan

In loving memory
of our friend Grace

The final part of this book contains a single dedication compiled from the 28 beautiful excerpts from letters to Grace in 2002 written by her friends and classmates of the Scoil Bhridé, Eglantine, Cork.

Though it broke our hearts to read them, they are a cherished collection of thoughts & memories about Grace that we will treasure as a Mum and Dad with all our family for the rest of our lives. A special thank you to the girls and their teachers.

Love and best wishes
Michael, June and family

Reflections from friends & classmates, excerpts taken from there 2002 letters
"In loving memory of our Friend Grace"

Dear Grace:

We miss you and your fun sense of humour, you brought laughter to our class, with your funny songs and games. You were a true angel, caring, loyal, kind, and fun, everyone loved you.

We miss your kind smile, a little flower in our hearts bloomed the day we met you, the fun we had together when you were alive, we will never forget. The way you used to wear onion rings as earrings and make us laugh and the way you always had something nice to say. Words cannot explain how much we miss you - we miss you more than a rich man would miss his treasure. We miss you more than the clouds would miss the rain, we miss your bright bubbly personality and your red rosy cheeks, we miss the way you lit up the classroom with your unbelievable humour, your smiling face will stay with us forever.

We all remember making our communion together, we stood proudly beside you while our class photo was being taken, your dress looked lovely, we were really hoping you would stay and make your confirmation with us.

We have so many memories of you in and out of school, remember all the parties you had, you always invited everyone in the class, making sure not to leave anyone out and there was always a massive bouncing castle, lots of sweets and fun.

Remember when you hadn't been well for a while and the principal came over with a card and a present for you, "Grace you were such a brave girl."

Now other people have the same disorder as you, and thanks to you, every one of them should survive. In a big way, you're a little hero, and now lots of other people won't have to suffer the way you did.

Last year on 12th November, your anniversary, we went out to the schoolyard and planted a tree with a heart shaped plaque underneath it to remember you. The plaque reads "In Loving Memory of our Friend Grace" and has two angels on either side of it. Even though all the girls at Scoil Bhride Eglantine are splitting up this year, it does not mean that on your anniversary we won't be thinking of you.

We know you are watching us, remember we love you, hoping you will not forget us. Goodbye Grace, our guardian Angel.

To Grace:

Last night I sent an angel to watch over you, It came back a lot sooner that I thought it would, and when I asked "why," It said," you don't send an angel to watch over another angel".

Stephanie Ryng

Goodnight!

Published by the Grace Nolan Foundation Ltd.
Limited by Guarantee.

Grace Nolan
AGED 7